(59.99)   T₁₇

THE PURSUIT OF INQUIRY

THE PURSUIT OF INQUIRY

Jay Schulkin

State University of New York Press

Published by
State University of New York Press, Albany

© 1992 State University of New York

For information, address State University of New York
Press, State University Plaza, Albany, N.Y., 12246

Production by Diane Ganeles
Marketing by Fran Keneston

Library of Congress Cataloging–in–Publication Data

Schulkin, Jay.
    The pursuit of inquiry / Jay Schulkin.
      p.   cm.
    Includes bibliographical references and index.
    ISBN 0-7914-1119-2 (hard : alk. paper). — ISBN 0-7914-1120-6
(pbk. : alk. paper)
    1. Philosophy. 2. Philosophy of mind. 3. Pragmatism. 4. Inquiry
(Theory of knowledge)   I. Title.
    B72.S33 1992
    144'.3—dc20   91-33859
                                                              CIP

10 9 8 7 6 5 4 3 2 1

To

April Oliver   *Robert Neville*   *Rosalind Schulkin*

Contents

Preface

This book reveals several lines of inquiry. The subject matter is diverse. And the contents lie across a number of disciplines. Therefore its text is interdisciplinary. In an age of such specialization as ours, this book is unusual; most thinkers tend to hide within their scholarly disciplines. But at the heart of the inquiring mind is the urge to go beyond the safety of one's trained enclosure.

My outlook and education, one should note, is from within both philosophy and the neurobiological sciences, and my philosophical stance derives from American pragmatism. It was, after all, the American pragmatists who emphasized inquiry and tended to tie it to the biological sciences. Their knot of philosophy and science was broadly tied. This book is within that tradition.

The origin of this book is to be traced to a seminar nearly twenty years ago in Switzerland with Erich Fromm. It was there that I became close to my good friend and teacher in philosophy, Bob Neville. He, along with my mother, Rosalind Schulkin, encouraged me in my pursuits of inquiry. Their worth to me is beyond measure and along with my wife, April Oliver, constitute my nucleus of meaning.

My colleagues at the University of Pennsylvania, a group of philosophers that met in my apartment over a five-year-period in New York, and colleagues elsewhere, continue to enrich my live. I mention several of them here, in addition to friends and family, that were helpful: Jim Anderson, Kent Berridge, Barbara Bettes, Ed Casey, Ted Coons, Ann Edwards, Alan Epstein, David Hall, Patrick Heelan, Paul Kleindorfer,

E.E. Krieckhaus, Jeff Lubin, Dan Marino, Bruce McEwen, Dick O'Keefe, Ellen Parr Oliver, Hal Pashler, Nora Peck, Alan Questel, Paul Rozin, Stanley Schulkin, Jon Schull, Ilana Snyder, Eliot Stellar, David Weissman, George Wolf, and Betsy Wood.

In particular, I thank two close friends, John Sabini and David Sarokin, who read every word more than once and helped me in all the important ways.

Earlier versions of chapters 2 and 9 were published in the journal of *World Futures: Journal of General Evolution*. An earlier version of Chapter 10 was published in *New Essays in Metaphysics*.

I have been supported during the completion of this book by a Research Career Development Award from the National Institute of Mental Health 00678.

The cover print is from the archives of the American Philosophical Society in Philadelphia. I thank Roy Goodman, Curator, and Eliot Stellar, President, for their help. The print, dated 1795, relates efforts to improve ship pumps. This society was founded by Ben Franklin, and is devoted to the study of practical philosophy.

Introduction

Philosophical inquiry is raw material for the art of living. At the heart of life are choices to be made; resourcefulness and good habits are essential. Life's precariousness demands good schemes to maintain balance and requires a sense of praxis, of putting ideas into practice, and relating them to the world.

In a difficult and confusing world, humans can still come to terms with life because inquiry reaches into everything, and human beings are natural inquirers. Importantly, there are different degrees of certainty or uncertainty, depending upon the kind of inquiry in which one is engaged. Inquiry is not tied to blind positivism, or detached rationalism, but grounded in mind, body, and discovery. The sense of inquiry is related to the existential real life dilemmas that we face. An inquirer realizes that expression is open ended and that existence is tied to action. Inquiry is an art, the way love can be an art. The discipline, patience, and, of course, intellectual acumen are our own doing. To be a good inquirer, therefore, takes effort.

The connective principle of philosophical inquiry is the idea that existence and action are tied together. But I believe that the existentialist overrates existence at the expense of action. And the classical pragmatist overrates action at the expense of existence. This book will demonstrate by the examination of choice and action that the two are bound together. The individual makes choices; but choices do not exist in a vacuum. The socially shared world imposes conditions on the individual, as does inherited biology.

The pragmatists emphasized both the social and biological context and appreciated that who we are is related to culture and biology.[1] They realized that the pragmatic is intimately related to the needs of the existential. It is tied to the biology of living things: it is connected to nature and it builds culture. Pragmatists also realized that conflict is inherent in life, and that freedom is not absolute. The pragmatists understood intelligence as centered in action.

The pragmatists (e.g., Peirce) also understood how beliefs guide action. They emphasized action not ideology, and, while they tended not to look inward, they did value experience and appreciate radical leaps that were grounded in what Dewey called "funded wisdom." They were not leaps into the absurd or irrational, as an existentialist might suggest were necessary. The pragmatists sought intelligent mechanisms in rational moments of discourse. They sought reason to predominate, but not at the expense of experience.

The existentialists turned inward and, in the same way as people do who look first out on the world and then in toward themselves, and are moved by what they see.[2] We have learned to look inward through epistemology, theology, and psychology. Contemplation and thought are tied to the inward turn. The mind is not passive and is not just a receptacle.

But the mind is essentially related to the praxis of life. The pluralistic universe that we encounter demands the pragmatic spirit. The pragmatist is attuned to the existential cries. The existentialist often exaggerated, forgetting about entrenched habits and funded wisdom that guide and organize our lives.

The irony is that the existentialists lacked a real sense of action (perhaps because they lacked a sense of inquiry) despite the fact that some suggested we also are "condemned" to act. They discussed and contemplated action, but often were impotent in the face of it, because they divorced themselves from the world. They were frightened in the face of freedom. But the pragmatists, mistakenly, tended to slight the insights that emerged from the turn inward.

The existentialists keenly saw the dilemmas of choice, which they often exaggerated. They generated a philosophy of action that was not rooted. While tied to choice, it was not tied to resourcefulness and intelligence. But both the existentialists and the pragmatists accepted that choices are embedded in conflict and that ideas in action are integral to a philosophy of life.

The early existentialists thought one could only be oneself when in opposition to the public, to social customs that mold the individual.[3] In the face of what is presented one needs to resist the seduction of the public. One turns inward to find oneself, to make oneself, to march ahead and to transcend oneself. The move is radical; chains are broken. The individual emerges. The denial of this choice factor is the "escape from freedom" or the common "bad faith" of humanity. This existential theme is developed in many of the following chapters.

Ironically, the polemic for the inward turn to "know thyself" (as the Greeks thought) ultimately came to mean a break away from the public. It meant losing the world, and in so doing the inward turn lent itself to idiocy: absolute privacy or madness. The existential inward turn seduces us to a world discarded.

Modern epistemology also encouraged the turn inward. Since the beginning of the modern era in the seventeenth century, knowledge has been the drama of the internal mind. With the downfall of both medieval scholasticism, and the authority of the church, knowledge came to be identified with what the individual constructs or legislates: the working authority of one's own mind. "Think for yourself" was the fitting dictum. Authority became internal, not external. This was true for empiricists and rationalists alike. For example, Locke, Descartes, and particularly Kant took the canon of reason to mean "think for yourself" in both knowledge and the legislation of morals. They argued that, despite an inner knowledge of the world, there could be agreement within the family of humanity. Thus, one went from the analysis of the internal to the legitimacy of the external; from the subjective to the objective.

Pragmatists tended to emphasize the role of the community and not what goes on in the inner workings of the mind.[4] We are social creatures who use social knowledge to construct reality. A theory of knowledge develops from the outside in; we learn the shared concepts of our communities and then we apply them to ourselves. The social world predominates. One looks to social and pragmatic discourse to resolve philosophical perplexities.

In life, the existential, or experiential, is as prominent as the pragmatic and the expression of action. In seeing the world as a place of choice, pragmatism also urges the guidance of action, providing coherence and order to the existential sense. The existentialist and the pragmatist should be attuned to experience, seeing experience as radical and to be lived. Through the discipline of inquiry, one sharpens these tools of pragmatism and existentialism.

Importantly, we are bound to the natural and cultural world. Our biology and political context determine the palette of our actions. The art of inquiry can enhance its colors. Both the natural and cultural climate, in addition to our early experiences, help determine what we are. Forced into the existential dilemmas of life, we do not know how free we are. We just act under the notion that we are free, to some extent, and we are (in varying degrees) resourceful in bringing our choices to fruition.

Humans contribute greatly towards saving themselves by understanding what counts in life and on being able to bring it about. Thus life is existential, and its trajectory is one of action; thus the pragmatic component. Choice is tied to action. It is existential in its call on the individual; it is pragmatic because the choices are tied to action and resolution. The dilemmas of choices are tied to the practices of life.

Philosophy should therefore open, and continue to keep open, the journey of inquiry. The philosophical spirit is not isolated from life, in an ivory tower or otherwise. Philosophical inquiry is concerned with the art of living—trying to live a good life—and the good found in inquiry requires preservation, as do all other fragile things. Here we find that the pursuit of the mind, the salvation of the soul, and the cultivation of the public are intimately connected.

As I indicated in the preface, my attitudes are within classical pragmatism, and therefore I should distinguish what

I see in pragmatism from what is seen by others (notably Richard Rorty).[5] But note at the onset, that this book is not a book about pragmatism and its history nor about the history of American philosophy, though there is a chapter (7) about it. What the book expresses throughout are common themes that were part of the fabric of classical pragmatism.

To say what I find in pragmatism, first and foremost, is the theme of envisioning ourselves as part of nature; continuous with other animals and part of the evolutionary process. Both James and Dewey were quite explicit in their recognition of Darwin, and the recognition of animal intelligence and experience. While Peirce tended to be Lamarckian, all three envisioned mind as part of nature. Mind's important function in nature is that of problem solving. That is, what animals do is try to solve problems; nature is replete with intelligent action and animal-human adaptations; but animals, like ourselves, are also curious and aesthetically oriented (chapter 8).

This view of pragmatism is very different from that of Richard Rorty. When he calls himself a pragmatist in his interesting and erudite works, he looks to literature and to *academic* philosophic disputes to bring his pragmatism to bear; his pragmatism is the dissolution of philosophic dilemmas. It is part of the general trend of getting therapies for one's maladies; philosophic perplexities need to be eradicated. Philosophy's ultimate role is to remove itself as a special discipline.

Rorty's heroes are Wittgenstein, Dewey, and Heidegger. Each, he claims, dissolved philosophy in one way or another. Rorty rightly construed inquiry as broad based and not dominated by one method and not scientific. He claims that no language community has in its possession something called truth. Moreover, construing the mind as representing reality is to be given up along with any form of essentialism. Instead of talking about representing reality it is replaced with talk about function, adaptation and coping. This much sounds pragmatic, even psychobiological. But when Rorty writes about "the world well lost" this is surely something Dewey would never say. It is too misleading. Dewey pushed inquiry to engage worlds, create them, cope with them, adapt to them, change them, and also represent them. Unlike Rorty, Dewey understood the real fact of what Peirce called second-ness; a sense of the world. The world is not to be given up, but rather engaged, or recovered.

Philosophy for Dewey is also not to be discarded but used as a license for engagement. *The Spirit of American Philosophy* is about meaning, ethics, esthetics, action, effort, learning, and will.[6] It is about creating communities, and participating wisely within them. Philosophy was not for the museum, but neither was it to be used for communities divorced from the contours of experience and their relationship to biological and psychological research. One must keep in mind that the classical pragmatists made contributions to the biological and psychological sciences, and their vision of who we are reflected that. Moreover, their tone was not academic. For all the elegance of Rorty, he is too academic. He acknowledges the contingency of life, and the empathy for others, particularly for their sorrow. But much of his discussion is not about the problems of life. Pragmatism I submit is about the engagement of life, and the vision of inquiry enhances that end.

Thus, inquiry for classical pragmatists would not be just the readjustment of sentences. And while pragmatism acknowledges that truth does not equal power (and is more than science narrowly construed), nor does it come close to literary criticism. Life problems are not literary criticisms of works. Pragmatism was never understood in that way, and shouldn't be. It is not as if literary criticism as a mode of inquiry is not important. It just does not define what phil-osophy is, certainly not pragmatism. Therefore, what Rorty leaves behind is the "hook" into the real. Classical pragma-tists engaged real problems, wrote about them. Philosophy was not dissolved through linguistic or philosophic therapy. Moreover, academic talk about anti-realism as the mark of the pragmatist sounds like bad pragmatism. This version of sophisticated pragmatism is an inquiry about words. In the end, it is infected with the disease of an overly exaggerated occupation of focusing on language.

The problem-solving abilities that evolved, and that are part of our psychobiologic abilities, are more than just about language. No doubt language expanded our abilities astronomically. But by rendering everything of importance as something about language we have shortchanged ourselves. Philosophy certainly requires clarity of language, and no doubt so does pragmatism. Thus when pragmatism loses its tie to the psychological and biological, and solely ties its concerns with coping and the adjudication of language communities, a lot of inquiry (and what we care about) gets lost.

Academic pedantic therapies for the cloistered are not of the rich tradition of classical pragmatism. Pragmatists were of the world, engaged it. Science figured prominently, but pragmatists understood science without being scientistic (or at least tended to) as the positivists were. A "reunion in philosophy" was originally thought to be the marriage of positivism and pragmatism.[7] Rorty in fact understands positivism to evolve and then terminate in what he calls pragmatism; the pragmatism of Quine or Davidson. But the vision of philosophy in the case of Quine is to dissolve all disputes into that of science, and a barren landscape amidst changing arrangement of sentences.[8]

In the pragmatic tradition cognitive competence, not just as language use, is an essential component in our problem-solving abilities. C. I. Lewis who thought of himself as a pragmatist continued a line that began with Kant;[9] how is knowledge possible? Pragmatists instead ask: how is inquiry possible? Categories of thought are presupposed (chapters 2, 3, 8, 9 & 10). Contemporary philosophers in Germany have fallen under the influence of Peirce and talk about what they call a "transcendental pragmatic perspective."[10] But American pragmatism is naturalized; the categories that provide order and the ability for competent problem solving evolved in the context of adapting to niches. The problem-solving abilities as Peirce, James, and Dewey understood, are part of our psychobiology. Thus the "theory laden view" of what we see and do (chapter 3), does not require that we lose our foothold in the world, by denying in elegant philosophical machinations the reality of it. So much sophistication a good pragmatist would avoid. Here Rorty, because he ties his version of pragmatism to the literary and sophisticated language use, departs from the traditional problems that engage philosophical inquiry within the American tradition.

As I indicated, my own philosophic vision of pragmatism engages the issues of choice and action, in the context of inquiry and the corrective method of experimentation (in some large sense of this term). One must recall that James founded the first experimental laboratory in psychology in this continent, and Peirce called himself a "laboratory scientist." Both men, as well as Dewey, worked on the empirical side of research. The practice of science was familar to them. And their philosophy was continuous with the findings in the biological and psychological sciences. No doubt had they been alive they would have integrated the findings of the neural sciences in their understanding of how minds adapted to and understand their worlds. James in fact already had begun to incorporate the insights of the brain in his great work "The Principles of Psychology." This was a work that Peirce himself thought was James' great treatise. As one looks at it today one sees the integration of philosophical issues within the purview of the psychological and biological sciences.

The pragmatism that I envision is utterly fallibilistic. It is tinged with realism in its approach to what it finds in inquiry. The pragmatism that I understand is not just about the continuation of a conversation in some specialized community of speakers. This should be fairly obvious by now. Inquiry, as I understand it, is tied to learning, with practical consequences. That is, the methods and the results of experimentation and investigations of inquiry are social (but not only social) in their consequences. Their justifications are placed in the community of inquirers for consideration. I suggest therefore that the laboratory method of self-correction in inquiry is what the pragmatists had in mind, and not the conversation of a philosophical elite.

In what follows, the first chapter places experience in the context of inquiry. The second chapter distinguishes the makeup of intelligence from rationality. Our present age tends to overvalue intelligence and to confuse it with rationality. It is, after all, wisdom that provides for the good life. The third chapter highlights the theoretical component of all emotions; all emotions are tied to thoughts. The fourth chapter is about what one learns about people when they are placed in several kinds of extreme situations. The fifth chapter makes clear that an integrated self and an "exercised will" are essential for the full expression of the soul—all one can be. The sixth chapter is about leadership in inquiry, and the social psychology of the members within it. And the seventh chapter is the exposition of the sense of inquiry developed within American culture. The eighth chapter ties choice, movement and the mind to the conflicts and resolution that emerge with aesthetic experience. The ninth chapter is about the evolution of the mind-brain, and the final chapter expresses a metaphysics of choice and action: the traditional problem of freedom and determinism.

Each chapter explores issues of choice and action and the pursuit of inquiry. The material cuts across a number of disciplines; notably, philosophical, psychological, and neurobiological. The mode of argumentation of this book is to present a point of view and convey its plausibility. The vector is slightly seductive, but the objective is to provide a coherent scheme to account for our experiences.

Chapter 1

Experience and Inquiry

Introduction

The tone of this chapter sets the context of the whole book. It begins with an analysis of why understanding other experiences is an important part of inquiry. It suggests that understanding other experiences is a hallmark of maturity. It argues that such understanding is not subjective but objective. Finally, the chapter suggests that an objective understanding of others' experience is the basic building block for the philosophical inquirer. This theme is therefore consistent with classical pragmatism and the active sense of experience as part of inquiry. The chapter then seeks to lay out part of what the discipline of inquiry is, and how it need not be a passive philosophical tool, but, rather, a lifelong challenge in all spheres of life.

Consider these points further. We live in an age that has highlighted the experiences of those living in other cultures. Airplane travel allows cultures to collide; television brings strange and alien imagery. Yet our temperament has tended to reduce experience out of the picture of knowledge (chapter 4). We so easily become entrenched in our own perspectives on the world that we exclude those of others. This occurs despite the fact that our media bombards us with different experiences daily. But our attitude is passive. This is because inquiry is not at the heart of the appreciation of other experiences.

Inquiry into the experience of others provide both the context and the content for moving beyond our own often narrow views of the world. And it may also be the case that our humanity is deeply connected to the consideration of experiences other than our own. Considering other experiences is how we move ahead; it is how we grow as we mature. Imagining other experiences is not only important for individual growth, but perhaps has broader implications for social policy. For example, imagining the life of a street person may be important in creating societal awareness on a broad scale for a more humane and hopefully effective social policy.

It is to some extent part of our psychobiological and cultural makeup to consider other experiences, and it is one of the fundamental ways in which we learn about the world (chapter 5). By placing inquiry into experience as something objective and part of the datum of knowledge, we enlarge our "universe of discourse." It also places the self-corrective method of inquiry and fallibilism as part of how to understand how we come to know one another and other animals. Thus it must be the case that our advances in knowledge are never to impoverish, and by cultivating inquiry into experience we expand our views on the world. But again, this practice is not one of being passive. Generating hypotheses, in the act of considering the experiences of others, is an active event.

I speak from the point of view of a practicing neural scientist and a pragmatist; classical pragmatism is an attempt to come to terms with our experiences: to make sense of them. Science, I believe, needs no defense. But when it is used to compromise our sense of matters of importance it is likely to be dangerous. Scientism is bad science, and is one consequence of trying to reduce experience from the purview of that which can be known. Our knowledge of how the brain works is not going to eliminate what we want to know about the experiences of other people, or animals (see chapter 9).

What we need is a large view of inquiry and of what counts as a testable hypothesis. This was the vision of the American pragmatists. We need to understand the experiences of those of other cultures, minority groups within our culture, and the great diversity of animal life. When experience is reduced to sensations or judgments as some philosophers have thought, or to behavior or neurons as others have thought, the consequence is misguided; the rich sense of the experience is omitted.

Appreciating the experiences of others is the major tenet of this chapter. We need to enlarge the notion of inquiry, objectivity and truth. The chapter begins with why experience is not captured by definitions, is not the same thing as the qualities that inhere in it, nor the judgments that one makes. Experience is also not identified with consciousness. Later chapters (e.g., chapter 9) address why mental events are not the same as what goes on in the brain.

Capturing Experience

There have been attempts to define experience in this century, but no one definition prevails. The experience of love differs from the experience of pain. No informative definition captures them both. A dog who has not been fed for a day experiences hunger, as would a human being. When rats or people taste table salt, they experience a salty taste. What common method or definition of experience captures the experience of hunger or of a salty taste? None, I submit. One point is that inquiry into experience need not employ one simple methodology or be circumscribed by one definition.

There is a history of thinking that experience is exclusively involved with sensory impressions (its qualitative intensity).[1] But experience is not simply a matter of sensory impressions. Consider this: An individual visits a cathedral that was bombed during World War II in England. What stands of the old cathedral is used as background for an outdoor theater. To the rear of the theater stands a new church that was built with the help of both the Germans and British. Inside, there is a sign that says that the church is open twenty-four hours a day, and there are also photographs of the holocaust destruction as well as the American bombing of Dresden. Part of the individual's experience is to acknowledge the destruction as well as the hope of this century. People destroy and yet rebuild together. Hope is the mortar of the new structure. This experience is not reducible to sensory impressions. No doubt there is a quality (or qualities) to the experience that should not be confused with the experience.

Another common mistake in interpreting "experience" is equating experience with an analysis of judgments.[2] The logic of this position is that our judgments are shared, not private. We can only know shared meanings of a community with its use of language.[3] We can know something about the way of life and how to communicate with others. But the judgments about what to do can be made by machines that do not experience, such as computers that make judgments daily. Experience is greater than the shared judgments that one makes.

Historically, behavioristic theorizing has dominated American academic psychology and philosophy. It no longer does, because in explaining behavior one is forced to attribute mental events as part of the explanation.[4] That is, it has become clear that it is enormously helpful to attribute beliefs, desires, and intelligence to intentional systems, as exemplified in chess playing computers, rats, or persons. In modern philosophical vernacular, the mentalistic attribution is an epistemological axiom. That is, we invoke beliefs and desires since we cannot predict or explain behavior without them. But there is no further inquiry into whether the creature (or machine) who believes and desires also experiences. The attribution of beliefs and desires to creatures like bats, apes, or persons can be independent of talk of experience. But there is, however, an *experience* of really *wanting, believing,* or *desiring.* Computers do not have that competence yet: that is why we do not care about them if we kick them, but do care if we kick a dog.[5]

Perhaps, the experience of intentionality can be found in directed bodily movements. At times when one intends to perform an action there are directed movements from which one ultimately does or does not receive satisfaction. For example, the Chinese dance Tai-Chi-Chuan has great form and intensity; intentionality pervades it.[6] The actions are performed with great intent. The body, in a well-patterned movement, is geared toward a goal that may terminate in satisfaction. The goal of each movement is explicit while the body is at peace, and yet attentive. These movements are intentional and the intention is part of the experience.

Attributing desires and beliefs thus is not everything. We also want to inquire further into those creatures that we believe embody those beliefs and desires, not just functionally but experientially. If one believes that there really are experiences and that no future language will replace them without including them, then one is committed to understanding them.

But for many contemporary philosophers and psychologists, the term "mental event" has been disassociated from its traditional use. One speaks in contemporary terms of mental operators in the same way that we would speak of the function of the kidney or the operations of the nephron. We do not think of the kidney as experiencing anything, and the same holds true for the "mental organs". These organs, e.g., the computational procedures involved in judging the trajectories of moving objects, in maintaining perceptual constancies, in generating sentences, or in the learning of skills, are not part of what we experience. Mental events, for the most part, are neither conscious nor experienced in this view.[7]

By contrast, in the more traditional view, mental events are part of experience. How the mind operates is akin to how we sense the world: the way we get around our likes and dislikes, emotions and associations, beliefs and desires. The mental is the essence of the subjective. All mental events are conscious and therefore a part of experience. We have learned that a large part of our mental life is unconscious (chapter 5). The result has been that experience is, or is seen as either less important, uninformative, or simply too difficult to study. And this I believe is a mistake, for as I indicated a large sense of our evolved humanity occurs because we can consider other experiences other than our own.

Are Experiential Events Difficult to Confirm?

Philosophical psychologists, like Fodor, have raised what has been called the "inverted spectrum problem."[8] That is, one could imagine two people who were alike behaviorally, but when shown an object and asked its color one would have the experience of red, while the other sees green. Nothing in their behavior would indicate any difference in their experiences while looking at the object.

When inquiry into experience is put into these terms, the study of experience may seem somewhat objective. It is true that although two people's behavior may be the same, with the same causal antecedents, the experience may still be quite different.

The inverted spectrum problem, however, is an important and challenging issue in the study of inquiry, but should not undermine investigation. There is indeed uncertainty about whether two people have the same experience. We could be wired in the same way, with the same causal history, and still experience differently. There will always be uncertainty in any form of inquiry. But we do have warranted assertions from convergent tests that lead us to believe the objective hypothesis that we experience many things in a similar vein. Thus we can know, and do know something, about the experience of other people.

We can even know something of the experiences of more primitive animals. So, for example, it is a warranted hypothesis that rats who are salt hungry experience something pleasant when they taste salt. When they are salt hungry, they display the facile profile that they would express as if the salt were sweet. They experience pleasure. This may also be true of people. People report that salty foods taste pleasant when they have been placed on a low sodium diet. By contrast, if they are replete with sodium they show distaste for salt.[9]

It has been argued that we cannot know what it is like to be a bat because the bat's construction of a world and its sensory system and experiences are so drastically different from our own.[10]

> "But bat sonar, though clearly a form of perception, is not similar in its operation to any sense that we possess, and there is no reason to suppose that it is subjectively like anything we can experience or imagine."

"Insofar as we can imagine this (which is not very far),
it tells us only what it would be like for us to behave as
bats behave. But that is not the question. We want to know
what it is like for a bat to be a bat. Yet if we try to imagine
this, we are restricted to the resources of our own minds,
and those resources are inadequate to the task."

Of course there is a similar, though less compelling,
objection with regard to one's knowledge of a fellow human
being. One can imitate another's behavior but one is still
oneself. To have your experience (so the argument goes) one
would have to be you. The experiences could be different even
though the behavior is the same—the inverted spectrum
dilemma. But pragmatists look for reasonableness and to
inquiry.

Consider a possibility: Suppose that it were possible to
rig up an apparatus that allowed one to hear sound in much
the way that scientists hypothesize that bats detect their
prey.[11] One's experience might then be, in part, something like
a bat's. The experience of detecting prey and getting around
by echolocation would then come to life to some extent. Still,
it may be too difficult to simulate. But if we put a person in
a situation, a bat-like domain, and he or she is able to detect
objects the way we theorize bats do, the latter would constitute
some evidence of a bat-like experience—just a bit. Theories
about the bat, formed in the context of careful observations
and supplemented by insightful experiments, lead to a
simulation of the purported world of the bat. Then we check
and alter, the same as we might do with an ape, person, or
rat, or at whatever point we imagine experience to emerge
in phylogeny.

It is indeed farfetched to imagine that one could do
everything a bat does. It is much easier to conceive of the
experience of the gorilla. We share more of the same biological
stuff. Still, while the experiences are not identical, a sense
of the bat's world can emerge for the human inquirer. A
community can reach agreement and speak coherently and
employ criteria. One can inquire into the experience, and it
is not foolish to do so. One can be a good inquirer, capture

and imagine quite a bit about other experiences, and test hypotheses. Moreover, the kind of direct demonstration for the bat's experience cannot be provided for humans.

A "falliblist", or pragmatic inquirer, is one who must face different hypotheses about a problem and choose. The warranted assumption is that there is a correlation between behavior and experience in creatures like ourselves. Although an inquirer might erroneously hypothesize about an experience, it is all done rather easily and can be tested. The question of whether one can capture experience correctly always remains. The skeptic can still object. In recognizing this, one should be humbled. This message is a reminder that the confidence wanted, or the certainty desired, cannot always be acquired—but should not block inquiry.

As I indicated, inquiry into experience, as it is construed here, is not a mere sensation or a judgement. Also, experience is not the same thing as consciousness. One can have the experience of being a Martha Graham dancer without being particularly conscious of it, nor can the reduction of experience to a neural field capture what it is to experience joy. In what sense do endogenous opiates secreted by the brain describe our joys and pains? Moreover, one can know all the causal relations about how one got to where one is without knowing one's experience. This is no substitute, since what one wants is to be understood in terms of the unique first person experience.

One can simply deny that there are experiences, or suggest that the term should be eliminated as frameworks change.[12] One can conceive of experiences as theoretical entities, but then they are a very well-entrenched set of concepts. It is very hard to imagine giving them up the way one would imagine giving up the concept of gravity or some other concept. Gravity is simply more removed than the experience of love. What they are removed from is simply what one experiences. Experiential concepts are deeply entrenched, they are not like ghosts. To deny them would require an unnecessary radical shift in our understanding of things.

Objectivity and Experience

Hypotheses are objective if they are testable. If warranted, a hypothesis ought to be agreed upon by a community of inquirers, because it puts forth the phenomenon in the best way possible, given the current alternatives (see also chapters 6 and 7). What counts as an objective hypothesis varies with the subject matter. An objective claim sometimes provides a sense of how something works, is organized, is predicted or is experienced. It is something that is always disputable or fallible, that is part of what makes it objective. One doubts a claim when there are particular reasons.

What are the characteristics of a good inquirer? One factor is that ideally, inquirers make themselves vulnerable by challenging the very beliefs they argue for. It is this vulnerability that marks the quest for objectivity more than making a case persuading. Making a case is one thing, being objective about a claim involves more. The vulnerability of objectivity should be voiced loudly. It is all too easy to deny the subjectivity of others. The barbaric tramples here. And we all do it. But nonetheless, objectivity can be reached about experience.

The most general feature of what one does when making an objective claim is giving a plausible story. One states one's beliefs (or those most likely to be challenged) and the reasons for the beliefs, making a case for their viability by persuading an audience of the merits of the claim and subjecting the beliefs to criticism. What is persuasive or warranted varies according to the subject matter. In one case prediction may be the persuasive factor. In another, it may be the perspicacious analysis of a text. In both cases, what makes it objective is that it can be criticized, tested, or challenged in some form. The inquirer makes a case to which the community of inquirers can respond.

But it is possible to predict behavior without referring to experience. But when it comes to humans or other animals one wants knowledge of experience. It is a quest to know what it is like for them to exist. Prediction is not the only measure of truth, or the only measure of understanding. The concept of understanding is larger than the notion of prediction. Simplicity is not the last word, and science narrowly construed is no Bible.

Now one might ask, "what kind of understanding do I have when I understand the experience of another? How is it different from other kinds of understanding—say of the way a hormone acts on the brain? What do I know when I know what it is like to be another?"

When one knows what it is like to be other people, or animals, one knows the way they experience their pain and sorrows as well as their joys.[13] One knows how they get about, how they respond to different people, what their interests are. One shares biological and cultural frameworks with others.

To understand what it is to be another we need to put ourselves into the other's shoes. This is accomplished by reconstructing the experience of the other. If the other is a scientist, for example, and we are interested in what she is like as an inquirer, we learn about her research—how she thinks and what she finds interesting. We watch her talk and observe the social self she displays to the community. We then rehearse for ourselves what it seems like to be her, and then we look to determine whether it is something similar for her. A case is made. Evidence is offered. Ethologists and anthropologists may do much the same, as do some actors, dancers, friends and therapists. The experience is conveyed, the life of the animal is presented, the internal is appreciated.

There is another issue. Often when we care about other people one of the things that we try to do is get a sense of their experience—not just what they do, but what it is like for them, how it connects up with their life history. Part of our capacity to recognize another as a person requires that we have a sense of her experience. When this is withdrawn, or avoided, so is the elegance and form of being human. In being human or civilized we recognize the experience of others. The view that inquiry should be broadly defined, and experience and its study be made empirical, was suggested by James early on.[14] Given access to the experience of other people makes it easier to love, forgive, care, and also to avoid them. This is not trivial.

The Commonplace

One often has a sense of the experiences of others. Consider what happens when one reads or hears reports of people's experiences. The communication of experience is taken so much for granted that it often goes unnoticed. Television, movies, books, and the media in general provide an account of the experiences of people. We want to know what it is like to be a great personality (a ball player, a ballet dancer, a musician). We voraciously consume tidbits about their lifestyles and life histories in order to find out how they arrived at who and what they are. Still the way we appreciate another person is by coming to see what they see, or at least getting some idea of it: that is, inquiring into their experiences.

The analysis of experience, in philosophical terms, is often analyzed in terms of the "what" and the "how." One kind of knowledge of experience is the "what" of a person, for example, the kind of dancer she is. The other kind of knowledge is the "how," the particular way the individual actually is. One knows not just the "what" but the "how" of the dancer. That she dances in a certain style of experience is "what" she is. "How" she dances is more indicative of who she is. The "how" is the ultimate goal. But in both cases one speaks of experience. It is the knowledge of the how that gives the confidence to say "oh yes, I know what she's like as a dancer, how she experiences being a dancer, how she relates to music, what her body expressed." Since the idea of her experience can be tested, challenged and corrected, it is objective and agreement can be reached. This methodologic and pedagogic distinction between the "what" and the "how" highlights a common-sense fact.

Knowledge, experience and its fruits have been put very nicely by an anthropologist:[15]

> "To some extent we are all prisoners of our own culture; traveling to other lands gives us a chance to break out temporarily and briefly taste what it is to be not just somewhere else but someone else."

The experience of the other and what it means for someone's life has been elucidated by the actress, Olivia de Haviland, who played Melanie Hamilton Wilkes in "Gone with the Wind."[16]

> "The character of Melanie Wilkes was the woman I always wanted to be. The role of Melanie meant a great deal to me; she personified values very much endangered at that time. The source of her strength was love. For a little while, as I lived her life, I felt her love, felt her trust, felt her faith, felt her happiness."

People other than actors take on roles, especially children whose lives are filled with play-acting. It is hard to imagine personal growth occuring without this capacity (a biologically and culturally important phenomenon).

The parochialism of one's own experience is liberated by appreciating the experiences of others. This is important for wisdom or rationality, as discussed in the next chapter. This is where inquiry into experience and wisdom meet.

Inquiry into experience is also important for an appreciation of other animals. In a zoo for example there is an old female gorilla who has spent a better part of her days in there. She is quite special in one regard; she knows how to upset the noisy intruders. She vomits up some of her food, or defecates, evoking a characteristic feeling of disgust in the onlookers. Then she looks at the crowd and, with what appears to be quite an intentional action, removes and eats the food from the vomit and feces to provoke yet a further cry of disgust from the crowd. Her experience includes the intentional thought of wanting them to experience revulsion. In fact, it is known that higher non-humans, primates, are intentional creatures (see chapter 2).

After conveying a sense of what the old gorilla is like, one can explain much of what she does and go on to predict her behavior. In this regard, some studies of the gorilla go to great lengths to give us a sense of their experiences.[17] One feels satisfied that one knows this creature when what is known is something about her experiences. The same holds for humans. To a lesser extent, the same holds for rats.

With regard to the issue of objectivity, part of what one means when one acknowledges the experience of others is that one can get to know them in part. And of course, one's judgments about each other experiences can be either correct or incorrect, as is true of all claims. How can one know which? As I already indicated, one would generate tentative hypotheses to convey the experiences, ones that seem well grounded, bear fruits, and can be checked, challenged, and replaced— which is what one does in all domains of inquiry.

Then what reason is there, outside of wanting only necessary knowledge, to doubt, as some thinkers do, the very existence of other experiences, or that we can have knowledge of them? One can be scientifically chauvinistic and deny that experiences really are objective, defining objectivity in terms of physical laws. This is both incorrect and pernicious. Or one can just be skeptical; this doubt is akin to doubting that there is an external world, or that if there is, one cannot know it at all. But in terms of justified belief rather than necessary knowledge, claims about experience can be justified. The skeptic asks for too much. In terms of truth telling, one has pragmatically warranted reasons for the belief that others have experiences of various kinds. One can reach agreement with others, and there are criteria for adjudication. Who seriously doubts this?

The skeptic reminds us of our ignorance. This is important. We do not want to slight the skeptic, but we allow her to sit and feel the impact of our shared experiences and knowledge of each other. The force of this phenomenon makes it more difficult for her.

Limits

Are there intrinsic limits to inquiry into the experience of others? There is really no metric for answering this question. For that matter, there is no metric for measuring how far the understanding of matter in physics can go. The lack of antecedently measurable limits is not troublesome itself, unless it is exploited by crude scientism.

If a person describes her experiences, unless one has a specific reason not to, they ought to be taken seriously. Sometimes psychoanalysis raises serious objections to the contents of the experiences, but to deny someone else's experience can be harmful and false. Thus there are limits to the knowledge one can have of what it is like to be another. If one presents a case for how someone experiences disgust and the person says "no, that's not it," then one is forced to believe her no matter how much contradictory evidence one has accumulated. The same is true with regard to the exhibition of pain behavior and the lack of experience of pain that a person might report. If a person reports that she still feels pain even though levels of neurotransmitters suggests she should not, it is hard to deny her. The doubt that lingers is one of the dilemmas of life and knowledge.

But people often feel that they are not understood. There is something about personal experiences that others cannot always capture. Saying that we do not quite capture a person's experience is akin to saying that one does not quite capture the real world. There is no proof of complete knowledge of the external world, or how close we attain truth in general. We do not have complete knowledge of anything. What we do have are specific instances, where we offer interpretations and where inquiry is conducted in a piecemeal fashion. If it is a good interpretation of a person or an animal, it conveys what is important to note, and the experience comes to life.

Conclusion

Inquiry into the experience of others is often undermined and has not been stressed enough as something to study and think about seriously in our culture. It is ironic that, in this century, inquiry into experience has achieved a kind of radical legitimization and understanding through the psychological, anthropological, and phenomenological inquiry.[18] We are for the first time publicly expressing theories of the existential—the life experience.

It is generally through the interactions with friends, parents, siblings, television, schoolyard, music, the study of literature, and of history, that the child first gathers a sense of what the experiences of others are like. It is not very often put into the context of inquiry. Most often, this is relegated to the subjective from an early age. So the expression "well, that's just your opinion" is often heard in this context as a way of indicating the belief that there is no objectivity to be gathered here. This is a common way of dismissing the event on the grounds that it is not real. This is both unfortunate and mistaken.

Inquiry into experience should be stressed. Why? There are important values associated with this kind of inquiry. These include the liberation from myopic or parochial points of view. An appreciation for the differences in experience may emerge. This figures importantly in being "rational," in being civilized (chapters 2 and 5).

What one does in the context of inquiry into others is to theorize and test with regard to their experiences. By considering other experiences we are forced to reflect on our initial perspectives on the world, our customs or way of life as one among many. As a result, objectivity about oneself and others is strengthened.

Pragmatists, like Dewey, made experience central to his philosophic vision.[19] And like James, experiences were not just passive and inquiry was extended to them. Moreover, this capacity to imagine the experience of others is a striking phenomenon. It is the hallmark of the mature, enlightened human. To have it in the service of objectivity and inquiry is valuable. Objective claims can be made about other experiences. Existential or experiential knowledge of the other is not legitimately satisfied until a sense of their experience is achieved; only then is there really knowledge of the other. By legitimizing the objectivty of knowing another's experiences, the natural sense of taking in these other experiences can be placed in the context of inquiry, discovery, and growth.

Chapter 2

Intelligence and Rationality

Introduction

Because of developments in the twentieth century in the use of language, "rationality" ought to be distinguished carefully from "intelligence." A wide gulf divides the old sense of wisdom—associated with rationality—from the functionalist sense of intelligence—associated with problem solving, IQ tests, and other algorithmic tasks.

With some justification from our inherited language, intelligence is taken to mean thinking through an issue or providing an explanation via the rules of thought, the actual inferences made, and the successful strategies displayed. Intelligence also has to do with making a world intelligible, and most importantly with solving a problem, or articulating a situation while using a hypothesis to solve a local problem.

The modern discussion of rationality is primarily concerned with intelligent action rather than with rational considerations.[1] Yet there is a common sense distinction between intelligence and rationality, which reflects the importance of reasoning and its use in human life. Classical pragmatists understood this fact.

The claim here is that rationality is aimed at the "good life," at a wisely lived, though not necessarily successful, existence. We have all known people who are pristine problem solvers—smart, working from rich frameworks, expert at valid inferences—but who do not do or care to do the right things in important situations. They have intelligence but not rationality. Rationality may lack facility at predicting the

27

future, a feature of intelligence, yet it is the habit of inquiring into the meaning and value of things, of being open to consider one's beliefs and those of others, and of subjecting beliefs to scrutiny. But the most important distinguishing feature of rationality is that it involves the consideration of ends worth pursuing because they enhance the quality of life, or, as Whitehead said, because they promote the art of "living well."[2]

There are four essential features of rationality. They are: (a) recognizing other minds while maintaining a healthy respect for the plurality of perspectives they exhibit; (b) trying to legitimate one's views in a public forum; (c) showing fairness to others; and (d) appreciating and interpreting the values inherent in things. This use of the term rationality comes from the speculative tradition of contemporary philosophy and from common sense.[3] Classical American pragmatism thus transcends the usual distinction between rationalism and empiricism.

The discussion here aims to contrast rationality with intelligence, and hence begins with a brief examination of a model of intelligence and ends with a discussion of rationality. The main thesis is that intelligence has to do with problem solving, while rationality has to do with wisdom. The distinction is important, because cultural advancement depends upon being rational or wise; one can be smart and be barbaric, but not wise and barbaric.

Intelligence in Biological Systems

Knowledge of the empirical world has become synonymous with statements about the world that are uncertain.[4] Animals like ourselves reason about probabilities in the face of uncertainties.[5] The foundations of thought center around the consideration of probability judgments. In ethological or economic terms, to reason is to generate values for action that are derived from the uncertainty of the costs and benefits (the values of the variables) that result from taking a certain step. The problem of induction is the problem of life. The world's regularities remind us of the stability of some of our beliefs.

Consider the behavior of a rabbit. She is thirsty, but the water hole is thirty yards from where she sits. She has a litter, and predators are abundant. We assume that she assesses the relevant factors before deciding whether to go down and drink; that is, she assesses the extent of her thirst, the needs of her offspring, the terrain and the distance from the water hole, and the chances of being preyed upon. She finally determines a best course of action and acts. Decision making is contingent upon the uncertainty of successful action (and in fact decision making is endemic, as discussed in the final chapter). The rabbit is considered intelligent insofar as she assesses all the relevant variables and finally decides on the best course of action. Knowledge plays a fundamental role in the rabbit's final decision. But it is not the "funded wisdom" of culture. The rabbit generates values for action in the context of considering various hypotheses. The action is guided by categories, or rules of problem solving. These are all aspects of intelligence, part of our evolutionary inheritance.

It is not surprising that learning devices within the rabbit respond to significant information by predicting future events. Knowing what is to come is a key feature of survival; so significant information plays a crucial role in communicative action.[6] The engaged semiotic is largely for the sake of predicting the future and solving problems in a contingent world.

Like us, rabbits generate hypotheses and test them, and then depend on some more than others. They are geared toward predicting the future. These are cardinal features of adaptive creatures.

Rabbits are not conscious of these mental events or feelings. As I indicated in chapter 1, psychological mechanisms, including affective ones, are largely unconscious. The act of walking through a door and the trajectory of one's body are outside of one's awareness; nonetheless, they are mental events. Similarly, the mechanisms responsible for learning the language of our culture and the events that make this possible are largely unconscious. The cognitive competence displayed in contrast to the paucity of conscious moments suggests that most of the cognitive mental life is outside of our consciousness.

This analysis of mental life characterizes organisms as cognitive devices (chapter 3) designed to resolve problems with strategies they often possess by nature's design. The rabbit employs everything it knows to try to satisfy its desire—getting a drink. The mental life discussed in some economic contexts is similar to that of the rabbit (except that in this domain stockbrokers are more conscious of their decisions). At the heart of human economic existence is ordering priorities, determining the probability of success, arriving at the best method to achieve it, then seeking satisfaction.

Thus the rabbit and the person share similar properties; both seek to satisfy desires and both have elaborate cognitive mechanisms. It takes great skill to avoid predators, care for young, build nests, communicate with others and remember maps of terrains. Intelligent systems are successful; they are the specific strategies to resolve environmental dilemmas which have been selected by evolutionary factors.[7] The animal has sets of specific learning or hypothesis testing mechanisms for the solution of specific problems. The hypothesis-testing mechanisms are prime factors of what one might mean by intelligence.

Consistency is also a striking feature of any such design; rabbits have to be consistent if they are to survive.[8] Consistency is an essential feature of logic and intelligence; without it there is chaos but with too much of it there can be dead habits and sterile action because of rigid thinking.

Artificial Systems

The designer of artificial intelligent systems thinks of the sort of capacities, or knowledge, the machine would require in order to resolve a problem. When one assumes the designer's stance to build these machines, one frames strategies. The more intelligent the machine the greater the capacity to solve problems, the more options or strategies it can draw on, and the more resources it has at its disposal. Intelligence is manifested through flexibility. For animals, one says that the cockroach is not as intelligent as the rat because it cannot resolve as many problems. The rat draws on alternative strategies that invoke a wider range of hypotheses to test. The same holds for the design of artificial intelligence.[9] Thus the range of hypothesis-testing mechanisms is a hallmark of intelligence and its evolution. The sciences of the artificial have not arrived at designing intelligent systems with any great sophistication. But artificial simulation research materializes our conception of intelligence.

Human Beings

Another example of what is meant by intelligent systems appears in the work of certain philosophers of science who, in the early twentieth century called what they did "rational reconstruction"—placing the results of scientific inquiry into a logical apparatus rich and clear enough to explicate the data and their meaning. These philosophers saw themselves as the guardians of thought. Reconstruction of scientific truth was identified with the logical form which explicated uncertainty in terms of frequencies. Moreover, logical form was an instance of convention, and one could be certain of a convention because it was a human invention. The rational structure consisted of the probabilities asserted by science. The rational structure guaranteed the value of a proposition. Logic was the new ground of thinking.[10] It made things intelligible. In this regard, logic replaced the transcendental. The new rules of reason were the moves within logic(s), so the logical apparatus was at the heart of inductive resolutions.

What is important is that the study of rationality, or what is called intelligence here, for the philosopher of science was construed as the explication of the logic of thought. That is, such a philosopher speaks of a logical apparatus, or a language of thought that is presupposed in making judgments and decisions. Without a representational system that embodies logical rules of inference, judgments or decisions of any kind would not be possible. To spell out the language of thought has now become, in part, an empirical endeavor.[11] Philosophers of science imposed logic. What all this amounts to in modern terms is that fundamental inquiry into the apparatus of intelligent systems, whether they be rabbits, machines, or philosophers of science, ought to examine the logical apparatus, i.e., the cognitive devices, presupposed in the guidance of judgments and action.

For clarification, one might look at it this way: In order to solve problems one presupposes a basic cognitive apparatus. The apparatus might be first order logic, but this has been shown to be doubtful. Whatever the language, what is important to note is that rational reconstruction is the transformation of information into a language of thought, taken to be the frame of all intelligent systematic thinking. This is what the philosophers of science were really doing, or should have been talking about. Thinking always presupposes logical machinery, a language of thought that is used to make judgments. The philosophers of science, like the rabbit, can't move without such cognitive devices. This is not to denigrate the philosophers of science, but only to draw the parallel between the intelligent system of the rabbit as it is used in problem solving and the intelligent system of the philosopher of science who uncovers the rules of thought which make problem solving possible. But the philosopher of science is not talking about rationality proper, except when talking about those things that are meaningful to pursue in intellectual discourse. This definition is too narrow; it does not encompass the pursuit of wisdom, the good life, and the moral dilemmas that we confront.

One final note on the issue of intelligence. When an animal is seen primarily as a decider, a probabilistic estimator, or an optimizer, and when the discussion is about humans, personality factors and their role in organizing behavior stand out.[12] For example, intelligent people will tend to be more reflective and less impulsive about deciding; they will weigh factors carefully. Rabbits probably do the same, but we assume that the personality factors are not very relevant in their case. The intuition is nonetheless simple and applicable to both; intelligent systems appropriately take their time, and exercise discretion. They are not rash.

The reflective problem solver or inquirer may also be a reflective person. This was Dewey's hope and one of the reasons why he labored for problem solving as pedagogy. Dewey always appreciated the role of evolutionary adaptations in problem solving, and saw the rudiments of human culture embedded in our problem solving capacities.[13]

Now the issue of rationality begins to show its face, and we lose the rabbit. The rabbit's world is dominated by questions about water holes, safety, and mating. The rabbit decides and then acts and its reflectiveness is limited. People not only anticipate the future, but at times limit their options.[14] And if reflectiveness is defined exclusively in terms of utility for success, then it applies to rabbits and people and would be integral to intelligence. If reflectiveness is elevated to its more lofty place—the intentional pursuit of actions to enhance the quality of life—then it enters the domain of rationality. Inquiry is the parent of rationality.

In summary, the cognitive strategies of rabbits, artificial systems, and philosophers of science constitute part of their intelligence. All of these disparate systems share the dilemma of problem solving. This is at the heart of a pragmatists conception of mind. The desire to reach satisfaction is also a striking feature of intelligence. It emerges from our biological makeup. The capacity to solve problems is fundamental to our existence, and inquiry is the method of survival.

Intelligence is Not the Same as Rationality

Historically, the concept of rationality is more fertile than that of intelligence with regard to the pursuit of the good and of what is valuable for life. Intelligence often has to do with the sophistic winning of an argument, not necessarily caring about the truth or what is valuable. Rationality breeds wisdom. The concept of intelligence does not have this feature either in an historic or a contemporary context. It has had little to do with knowing what is important. In one form or another, intelligent action has signified pristine problem solving, except for Dewey, for whom the concept of intelligent action had much to do with the enhancement of life.[15]

The common person distinguishes between the two quite naturally. For example: "Do you see my friend over there? He sure has intelligence all right but if he would use it wisely—he could be something." The rational person chooses the better course of action because it enhances the quality of life. Intelligent people are smart but not necessarily wise, and wisdom and its attainment are necessary to be rational. When the distinction between intelligence and rationality is overlooked, something important is omitted. Wisdom enhances the quality of life and provides the force behind cultural advancement.

Rationality is tied historically to the Socratic part of philosophy. Reasoning, or thinking, was not simply problem solving, but part of the reflective life—the good life. That was the goal of thinking. In the modern age thinking is defined more narrowly. Part of philosophy asks what is important in life, i.e., which path should be pursued and why. It reminds us of what is important, and is the search for the valuable, the worthy. But, having said what is meant by intelligence and having distinguished it from rationality, we turn to a basic mental feature tied to our biology which is presupposed for the achievement of rationality.

The Intentional: Bridging Intelligence and Rationality

Rationality emerges in creatures who can achieve the mental life of high-level intentional stances. This bridge between the intentional and the rational is largely manifested through social intelligence, which is essential for leadership (chapter 6): the more socially intelligent, the more intentional, thus the greater the possibility for rationality.

Intentionality is a biological phenomenon of many animal species which is essential for the evolution of intelligence. An intentional stance enables one to understand the action of others by attributing beliefs, desires and other mental events when explaining or predicting their behavior (chapter 1). Another factor to being an intentional creature is the sense in which these attributions are structured by thought. Thus the more intelligent the animal, the greater the intentional competence. When one person acts in such a way that another can know her beliefs and desires through intentional acts, they are both acting in a high-level intentional manner.[16] They are aware of a shared access to each other's intentions. The level of reciprocity and communication is striking. They both know what each other knows; they know it together. A shared world emerges, the extreme of a high level intentional act.

As shown earlier, other animals are also intentional. Evidence suggests that chimpanzees sometimes view their world in terms of the beliefs and desires of others.[17] A man reaching for an object that's beyond his grasp will be understood by the chimpanzee. The chimpanzee will select the appropriate object to aid him. The man wants the object and the chimpanzee recognizes his desire and helps, or not, depending upon whether she cares for him.

But human beings are the glory of intentional creatures. That is why much emphasis has been placed on trying to understand intentionality. The basic way we inhabit, and have a world, is intentional. It says something basic about us and the kind of animal we are. We may not be the only creatures that understand each other in an intentional way but we certainly do it to the greatest extent. While bees and other insects display a sophisticated kind of social responsiveness, the range of social behaviors is quite small and rigid, and is not viewed as highly intentional.

Perhaps a good anecdote of intentionality is when a father asks the intentions of the earnest suitor before letting his daughter out the door. The intentionality stated becomes one way of being socialized, and in this case a code of honor. His expectations and promises are his signature.

What does this mean? As the classical pragmatists understood the more we see our fellow humans in terms of their aims and expectations, beliefs, desires, and attempts to achieve satisfaction, the more we understand what they are. This is social intelligence, common-sensically thought to be the highest form of intelligence—the capacity to interpret others by attributing the right intentions to them. It is expressed when recognizing the beliefs and desires of others, and of course by being right about them, and when intention-ality plays a major role in the human mental life, an under-standing of others grows. The intentional is not the same as the solipsistic and the private, but reaches prominence in recognition of a shared and public world. Social intelligence, as we humans live it, is then manifest. An irrational person fails to recognize the intentions of others. Once we recognize the beliefs and desires of others, our view of them may change. We can appreciate their needs, aims, expectations, plans, and projects. Social intelligence allows us to pick up the right cues, see the other clearly. When we consider other views, the rational can emerge. The world is more than egocentric wants or needs. Others exist. In such a context we weigh and contrast different points of view; we capture the frame of the other, or the experience of the other, as discussed in the first chapter. This requires the dialectic of social interchange and may result in less barbaric behavior (chapters 4, 6).

This is important because, in the human social world, acts of rationality sometimes emerge when trying to understand others when disagreements exist. Disagreements in a plural-istic free society are pervasive. Empathy is essential in a civilized world. Parochialism is shed, and ideally, the question of worthy ends becomes the focus. The recognition of the intentionality of others—their beliefs and desires—lends itself to the pursuit of worthy goals.

Pragmatists undertand that it is in the social world that the rational discussion of ends emerges.[18] The Greeks, though exaggerating the claim, were right that privacy lends itself to idiocy. But as Socrates also taught, a rational mind also stands alone at times. This was also part of the revolt against medieval scholasticism, and requires thinking for oneself. As humans we have the competence for social intelligence, with high-level intentional stances as the basic preconditions. The understanding of others and their culture depends on it, as does the existence of a culture.

Rationality

Several prominent features figure in the evolution of a person's rationality. The first is that others be taken into account, that one sees one's view as one among many. As a rational being one is able to recognize that the "better" perspectives and experiences may lie elsewhere. One may realize that one's own experiences are impoverished. Secondly, the legitimation of one's view requires a public, social world. If the public is shut off, so is life in some deep way, and so is rationality—though one can retain segments of rationality without a public. But then it is reduced to the level of idea, which often requires a public for expression. The third factor is that people are more just when they distribute goods and when they consider the perspective of others. Others are desirous of the goods, and the scarcer some goods, the more likely there will be havoc. These destructive capabilities are partially avoided by coming to recognize the value of others— the fourth feature. A philosophical life glimmers. Consider further these four features of rationality.

Intelligence in the Service of Rationality: Recognizing the Others' Experiences

The problem solver who insures civilization and its evolution begins with the education of coming to see others and him or herself in the social world. He or she may then act fairly towards others when their views, values, and experiences are recognized. One comes to see one's own values or views existing as one among many. The problem solver confronts real life and important problems. Rationality demands a vision that is pluralistic—a society of thinking people living together. As Dewey understood, education, in the widest sense, delicately nurtures this possibility.[19] The end pursued is a pluralistic and cultured democracy with shared and funded value experiences. This is a context where the recognition of others and the appreciation of differences predominates.

Intelligence should be guided by rationality; it is integral, not in opposition, to it. We should use intelligence "wisely." One needs to be intelligent to achieve rational ends. The first step is a recognition and respect for other plights, a sign of civility and a step away from insularity.

Legitimation: The Public, Oneself, and the Other

The rational person desires self-knowledge, because one finds out about oneself by examining the world and one's part in it. The Socratic goal of life as self-understanding and the modern conception of legitimation merge. One comes to know oneself by coming to understand the world. In understanding the world there are moments of bringing beliefs forward, testing them in praxis against the world.[20]

The rational person gathers important knowledge of himself through disciplined inquiry. He has some idea of how he got to where he is and, possibly, where he ought to go next. Reflection is at the heart of such action. There are quiet and not so quiet moments of self-reflection, but the public is almost always omnipresent. This is not to reduce rationality to the public, but being rational is embedded in culture, and as we come to recognize the social conventions that we live by, human responsibility emerges, or fails to. Critical reflectiveness allows for understanding one's beliefs and their consequences. If responsibility then emerges, it is rational. Such legitimation is at the heart of a rational being.

Appreciating pluralism in a context of self-presentation is an important step in the evolution of cultural advances. Acts of reflectiveness brought to a public arena are acts of legitimation. These acts are transactional: they involve others. As I recognize your intentions and you mine, I legitimize my query and concerns as you do yours. The case is public. We legitimate our beliefs by making them public and exposing ourselves. This is an ideal of civil discourse and the labor of human ingenuity is well worth its placement here. This leads us to wrestle with the concept of justice.

The Ethical and the Polis

Perhaps inquiry leads us to see justice as the moral component of rationality. One component of fairness is the distribution of the goods of life in a way that shortchanges the poorest the least.[21] In a civilized or rational culture, fairness seems a necessary precondition. It may reduce human greed which all too often has no satiation. It does not have to undermine the competitive and hearty spirit of our biological natures.

As Rawls suggested, one way to make fairness a part of justice is shown in the following: when one's possible position in a situation in which some goods are distributed, is not known and one may be in any one of those positions, a sense of fairness may emerge because the uncertainty of one's position in the outcome motivates a greater attempt to equalize the share. To the extent that all of us do not know our positions, we may tend to distribute goods more fairly. No one wants to risk too much or end in the worst position, no position is going to be bad. Safety prevails. It is not out of any great love that these fair acts emerge, but out of a desire not to come up short. This would be true for many of us, but there are *just* people who would distribute without such extreme conditions. But people often do not risk much, and many do not mature or develop a healthy sense of autonomy and take up the reins of responsibility. This much also seems true—at least up to a point. Given these psychobiological constraints, one tries to establish conditions in which people would act fairly, or justly, toward one another.

The evolution of rationality, in contrast to intelligence, means going beyond crude egoism to recognize the life plan of others as being pivotal for one's own attainment of happiness. Realizing one's own life plans requires that one recognizes those of others. One way to do this is to recognize their experiences. This endeavor as James illustrated is empirical. One consequence is that the reciprocity of respect that may emerge is an essential feature in moving beyond crude egoism. This may emerge in considering the life plans of others.

Axiology

When we consider the experiences of others, these facts have values of one kind or another. The valuational traverses all life. We all transgress in recognizing the values in things, for example, failing to respond to the beauty, truth or justice of a person, or disfiguring nature's resources. But the dawn and crowning feature in the evolution of rationality is valuation. High-level intentional stances, a factor in the evolution of intelligence, are the preconditions; the consideration of the values and ends of others is only possible in creatures sophisticated enough to achieve such intentional stances. Social intelligence employs the intentional; the possibility of recognizing value is the result.

Valuation is at the heart of human judgment. This point was championed by pragmatists as diverse as C. I. Lewis, Dewey and R. C. Neville.[22] To be at all and to be appraised, interpreted, is to be of value. The question is, what kind? That, of course, varies enormously. There is no simple answer, but what seems clear is that value exists in fact. So in recognizing the other the value of the other comes to the fore, and in legitimizing myself my own value makes its appearance to the other. Similarly, the value of fair distribution makes its mark in the pursuit of acts of justice. Thus value is at the heart of being and its recognition is essential for rationality.

Four Features of Rationality

Four features of rationality have emerged from the discussion, each of which may be essential for rationality. The first is the appreciation of pluralism, the differences among us being recognized and respected; education of character is the goal, the use of intelligence is the dominant tool. The second feature is the legitimation process. We make our beliefs and desires public, bringing them to an arena and making a case for them. Civility bares its mark as it makes its stamp in culture, a culture catholic in its pluralism. Without a public in which to make one's appeal, tyranny and decay are the voices heard. Solipsism is deadening. Rationality is public and, by being public, legitimate. The third feature speaks of justice as fairness. Living together requires that we act justly towards one another: distribution of good(s) is employed as a means of enhancing the quality of the many. An imperative to be fair is made manifest in an egoism latent, but dismantled. This helps generate justice, and so it is good. And, finally, the fourth feature of rationality is the appreciation of the value that "inheres in things" to borrow a phrase of Locke's. An axiology of being is at the heart of this concern. To be is to be a value of one kind or another. There is no abstraction of value from fact but the recognition of this requires cultivation.

Why should one accept these principles? Because they seem to capture many of our intuitions about what constitutes a rational life, or how we might achieve one. Without pluralism and its appreciation there is the threat of tyranny; without a public with vulnerable legitimate individuals there is the danger of idiocy and the breakdown of the community and civility; without acts of justice in distributing fairly, dominance by disproportion reigns; and, finally, without an appreciation of values, vulgarity thrives.

Chapter 3

Thoughts and Emotions

Introduction

The central thesis of this chapter is that the emotions are embedded in thoughts. The idea that passions are passive, without thought, is related to the traditional mind-body problem. A body pulled about by passions is passive and reflexive; a mind is thoughtful and active. Hence the split between the noncognitive and cognitive.

The view I favor envisions mind in body, where bodies are active and not passive. As a *pragmatist,* cognition is recognized to be inherent in problem solving, in choice and action. In fact, cognition is a basic psychological fact that permeates everything we do. That is why the term "theory ladenness" captures a basic truth; what we see is always relative to a background theory or system of thought. Recognizing this may have therapeutic implications; to engage someone and to offer change as a possibility is to suggest a new way of thinking. Therefore, the capacity to think, traditionally tied to our sense of freedom, captures a basic truth. But while thought predominates, the world says no to some hypotheses and yes to others. A sense of the world independent of our thoughts is important.

Traditional and Modern Views of the Passions

The root meaning of passion is that of being in a passive state, or a state of being blindly led about.[1] To be in such a state is to be caused by something outside oneself. Passions are traditionally characterized as outside of one's control. Passions "happen" to one.

By contrast, to be causative is to be active. Mental events are causative; the passions, because of their passivity, are not active. Since passions are not self-generative, they are not active. They are not tied to agency. The passions are tied to movement; they are more like secondary properties— epiphenomena of kinds.

This brief characterization of the passions makes them seem not worth having. Thoughts are worth having because they are self-generative and active. Thoughts express the essence of mind—one's freedom and what is most distinctly human.[2]

Thought and freedom are considered essential human attributes. According to some, this is what makes us different from animals.[3] Animals are only passive—pushed and pulled about; they are guided by tropisms, or reflexes in modern terms. We are active because we reason—we think. Animals do not. Humans have minds, animals do not. Reason is distinguished from the passions. Animals are full of passion— animal passion. Humans are often "animal-like," but it is a privation and to be avoided. To be swayed by passion is to stray from reason and what is distinctly human, and to lose the strength of freedom, since freedom is tied to reason or thought.

Losing reason, then, is a bit like falling from grace. To be human and free is to be uncontaminated by the pulls and pushes of nature—desires or passions—as far as possible. One should avoid the passions and the passive state of being driven from without. The body is unworthy, not worth cultivating. The body is tied to passion—exploding in anger, becoming delirious through desire, bemoaning the gluttonous and the insatiable. The body weakens and it renders one passive; it provokes passion. The recognition of this fact can force discipline and temperance, or a denial of life. Both strategies deny desire—the body starves.

This line of reasoning goes further: when free of bodily constraints, self-creation or self-determination can emerge.

Spontaneous moments of self-determination express one's existential decisiveness (see chapter 10). They are true moments of mind and acts of potency. Within such moments true knowledge appears and places one beyond the shapeless sense of faint or confused images of ordinary life which are tied to the body (chapter 9). The human knower's self-generated activity transcends the confused sense of the body. It is reason liberated from the body.

To continue explicating the traditional view, reason lies within one, passions do not. Passions render images seemingly true through magical delusional moments.[4] Reason uncovers truth by looking inside—to its own source and free from imposed passions. Reason legislates from within.[5] The authority is internal, not external. The turn inward provides rationality, and universal features of humans are revealed. The inward turn provides the commonality among thinking persons which is freely arrived at since it is internally generated. The passions, by contrast, only offer ignorance, passivity, and diseased being— a turn away from a community of civilized thinking persons. Passions are subjective; reason is objective. Civilization rests on reason. Reason solidifies; passions provoke chaos or death.

These conceptions helped erect an historic mind-body problem. Mind became identified with thought; body became identified with passion. Mind was private, body was public. Mind was inner, body was outer. But these inherited notions have been criticized by many inquirers[6] and the resultant epistemology and metaphysics is faulty, misleading, and confused.

The view in this book sees animal bodies embodying thought; mind is within the animal body. The traditional dualism is undercut by, among other things, modern psycho-biological principles that uncover thought in animal action. In fact, thought organizes action.[7] Once one replaces the traditional distinction of active minds and passive bodies with minds organizing bodily actions by design, then the passions are not passive, brute and without thought. Moreover, one can be passionate and still be an inquirer. In fact, at the heart of any inquiry is passion—the passion to develop an idea, to see its value, implications, and even truth.

Physical Stuff

The passions, or emotions, are often tied to "nervous juices" that get secreted by different parts of the nervous system, or what the nervous system controls. These juices are secreted when the world upsets or impinges. The secretion of the juices is brutely physical and the result is a passion, simply triggered.

We often think of the emotions as the "juices going." When we "neurologize" we reduce passions to the nervous juices—the chemicals of the nervous system.[8] In fact the biological significance of the emotions has long been noted.[9] One of their prime functions is for communicative purposes with conspecifics, and for problem solving. Moreover, a range of emotions are expressed early in life, with facial displays figuring prominently. The visceral nervous system from cortex to peripheral autonomic ganglia is known to play a role in the organization of the emotions (chapter 9). But emotions, like other mental events, are not the same thing as nervous juices. Conceptions of the mental are disassociable from physical systems that instantiate them (see chapters 9 and 10).

The criteria, however, for distinguishing emotional from nonemotional thoughts will not be based solely on whether one is "hot" or one is "cold." The autonomic nervous system may be the main brain tissue mediating the emotions in animals like ourselves, but if emotions are mediated by autonomic juices, then they are "thoughtful juices."

Still, emotions are often brute-like and irrational (as are many of our thoughts). Despite this, they are embedded in a psychological framework and thus are part of thought.

Cognitivism

There are no "bare" emotions. They are not pure. We have become used to abstracting thoughts from emotions in our talk. There is an analogous phenomenon in the notion of pure sensations or the given.[10] The concept of qualia is used in describing the given of experience, or the qualities that we receive from the world. The reception of the qualia was passive. One just takes them in wholly with no choice in the matter. The idea is that the world causes these qualia which are then received and transformed. The qualia go from the pure and given to the judged, from the passively received to the actively thought.[11] The given is transformed by the application of concepts. The mind shows itself. It decides about the given, about the emotion; order is achieved, the chaos of the given is mediated.

The qualia, which came from without, seem to be to passions what judgments are to reason. Judgment comes from within. Qualia are imposed. Judgments are self-generated. The former speaks of the passive, the unformed—in Aristotelian terms, as potential matter for thought to form it. Matter is pliable, thought forms. Thought is active. Matter is passive, like clay to be molded. The distinction is deeply rooted and longstanding.

Consider the eyes. We think of visual input as being continuously transformed as one ascends from the retina to the visual cortex.[12] It is as if, at the level of the retina, the world is purely received. The image is pure and caused from without—the pure qualia. But it is not pure.

From the retina—which is brain tissue—right up through the visual cortex, visual events are interpretive. The visual system, like other perceptual systems, reaches out to the world actively.[13] There are no noninterpretive perceptions. Perceptual systems are designed to interpret. This provides the necessary order for action and accomplishment. At best one can speak of degrees of interpretation, or "theoreticity."[14] But what is true is that the retina selects and interprets relative to a background framework, as do the lateral geniculate and visual corticies, which are centrifugal in organization (chapter 9). All perceptual systems work that way, and so may the emotional systems. As the classical pragmatists understood, seeing is always interpretative.[15] Thus, thought is omnipresent.

The split between qualia and thought, or emotions and reason seems false on a number of fronts.

Even the experience of pain is theory-bound. The design of the pain system is embedded in psycho-physical judgments, which are always embedded in theories or networks of interpretations. In the case of pain, it seems as if there must be a low degree of theoriticity. Pain is more basic, more concrete, more unmistakable. But remember that what is concrete is itself theoretical. The notions of the abstract and the concrete are themselves inherited and theory-bound.

Since theory predominates, one should speak of the continued pragmatic use of a theory as being entrenched.[16] Those terms deeply entrenched in our understanding of things would require a big push and a lot of justification to be discarded. Can you imagine discarding the concept of pain? I cannot. And I cannot have a pain without a psychological pain system that allows for it. The pain system embodies the capacity to recognize pain. To recognize pain is to make a judgment: for example the onslaught of danger, which is the biological basis of pain—to inform the animal of injury. Therefore, the experience of pain is embedded in thought.

Thus pain and other emotional experiences, as well as the passions are embedded in judgment because we take in the world relative to a background framework. This is both a profound and trivial point. The world for us as knowers is always ordered and relative to a perspective. Thus, in some sense talk of qualia, or of the passions, is talk of judgments—interpretations—being made. Emotions, then, are judgments of certain kinds.[17]

Thus there seems to be an asymmetry; while it is suggested that there are no emotions without thoughts, there are thoughts without emotions. Mathematical reasoning and other kinds of formal reasoning do not entail emotional judgments, although emotions may play a role as motivating or triggering factors. We build computers that judge, but that do not feel. Therefore, all one can do is talk about different kinds of judgments—emotional, aesthetic, or simply computational. But it all involves judgments.

As Dewey labored to undercut it, this distinction between the noncognitive and cognitive is entrenched in our understanding of human behavior. It emerges in a variety of contexts. We have built our sciences and common discourse around the distinction. Someone tells us "you think too much—feel, don't think," and sometimes we hear the reverse.

Emotion is supposed to be unmediated and pure, thought is mediated. Emotion is supposed to be receptive, thought is constructive. But the discourse is wrong and misleading not because some of us are not detached from our emotions, or embedded in them. It is often said that there is an act of just seeing or experiencing unmediated. But again to see something is to have a perspective; that is, a framework is presupposed that structures and is necessary for the seeing. While the emotion is not reduced to thought, one cannot feel without thinking. The question is, how should one think while feeling, and how does it play a role in inquiry? This is its "cash value." This is one of the problems of life. Consider a therapy that deals with this issue.

Therapy and Theories

There is a therapy that is cognitive in orientation. It tries to change how people think.[18] The roots of the therapy are familiar: thought determines reality.[19] To change the thoughts is to change the experience. This therapeutic approach posits that the mental fabric is essential because experiences are embedded in judgments, so in order to change the experience, you have to change the judgments.

The therapeutic value of such a stance is difficult to evaluate. In some contexts it does not matter what one might think if the underlying physiology is deeply sick. Wishful thinking can be just that. But it is somewhat effective with people who are depressed, and it stands with other therapies, as one among many.[20]

But the therapeutic approach expresses a basic truth. All emotions are embedded in a psychological perspective, or theory. Depressive people theorize about the world and about what to expect, and these theories determine, in part, their experience.

One might envision further that the frameworks of emotional judgments are essentially modular. This is an empirical issue. It appears that many forms of thinking (spatial, temporal, statistical) are modular in scope.[21] Thus there may be highly specialized principles applicable to emotional judgments. There may be one framework for the judgments in anger, one for those that are a part of friendliness, etc. The emotional frameworks are to be understood as having specific properties. Therapists would focus on the perspective to be changed and would provide new ways of seeing. In doing so, new ways of experiencing could emerge. Thus, while the mental is no longer tied essentially to the conscious and alterable, all emotions are nonetheless embedded in thought.

Freedom and Idealism

Turn now to two philosophical issues: freedom and idealism. They are both relevant to the discussion because freedom has traditionally been tied to thought and thought is tied to philosophical idealism. Consider freedom first.

We are not unconditionally free (chapter 10). There are real-life constraints. A conception of radical freedom drives some to "nausea" for all sorts of reasons.[22] Radical freedom is difficult to bear. This freedom allows for no constraints, not even unconscious ones. By contrast, a conception of freedom within constraints corresponds to our sense of experience. The world and the mind impose limits by setting order. The mind also posits possibilities. In so doing, it is at once free and determined; the determined part sets the conditions and the free part makes the choices within this order (see chapter 10). At times there is no choice, because there is often no person present, no person in control. Very often what one finds are sets of parts assembled together in well orchestrated habits. There are degrees of freedom in a literal sense. To believe in radical freedom is absurd; it is just as absurd as the conception of unconditional determinism. One view posits radical, unconstrained freedom, the other brute unthoughtful passions—one is mental, the other physical. One finds oneself in an unfortunate abyss in adopting either position.

Like Peirce, James, Dewey and other earlier pragmatists, I believe one should place the mind in nature, which is central in organizing experience and behavior. There are psychobiological constraints on all organisms including persons, on what they can experience and what they can know. No one knows how to give live values for many of these variables. The valued facts are partly open for inquiry, and some hypotheses are more warranted than others. The situation is not hopeless for inquiry—just difficult.

The truth about passions is that they are at once chosen and brutish. How much of one or the other it is difficult, close to impossible to say. But I believe that some judgments are so highly constrained that it makes no sense to talk of responsibility for their expression, or to suggest that they can be altered (chapter 5). Still, even for cases like love it certainly makes sense, and seems true, that choice plays a role. But the use of the word "choice" here seems pushed. One feels that the love is triggered and passionate, of the visceral mind. It is, but it is embedded in a framework and there is an element of choice. Thought is required and with thought there is some freedom.

The decisions being made reveal a choice factor, but it is a realm without a clear metric. Nonetheless, it is unreasonable to assert that all emotional judgments are chosen. This is truly absurd and false. It is the kind of absurdity that Sartre found worthy and deeply ontological. While ontological responsibility is the price of humanity, falling short is also the essence of humanity. Critical common sense posits a middle road between the bruteness of determinism and the nakedness of freedom (chapter 10). There is no compelling reason for either extreme. What one needs are ways of coming to understand the degree to which there are genuine choices in emotional matters. This, in part, is empirical.

By claiming that emotional judgments are not solely passive, one introduces responsibility. There is ontic responsibility—for things—but within constraints. The result of constraints is order. Though the passions are just that—passionate—they are not necessarily brute or passive. They are certainly not without the mind's ordering, and are sometimes somewhat chosen.

Now turn to the issue of idealism. The question is, if everything is relative to a perspective (idealism) how can we know the real (what is independent of perspective)? First, there are more things in the world than what we can know. There are epistemic limits to us. Moreover, real things exist despite the fact that it is all mind-dependent for us as knowers. Critical common sense—pragmatism—suggests this.[23] One should take the real as an entrenched hypothesis, which is itself a judgment, despite the fact that the "long run" agreement of truth is a myth. The theoretical leap of positing the real bolsters our epistemological concerns. A conception of the real ties our actions to ideas that resolve conflicts. When nature says no to an idea it rejects the plan and action; this is what Peirce called "secondness." The real secondness is itself a warrant for belief. The point is that it is not all make believe or magic. Men and women are different. Rocks are hard. Tables are in the room; we bang into them. No one denies this, except some philosophers and mad people. The real is a primitive concept, and very entrenched.

As a knower, one posits reality. Nature has made animals like ourselves hypothesis testers, with theories that guide action. The mental architecture is elaborate. Hypotheses get rejected and accepted as the real shows its face. The real rejects and mildly accepts. There is convergence, truth, and something like the growth of knowledge; our theories terminate. Undoubtedly, the termination is in the real. The metaphysics seems sound. The goal is to be reasonable; to deny the world is not. To say we have direct access to the real is also not reasonable. But while the real is posited, it is hypothesized that nature constrains our theories. The result is that some theories are validated, while others are not. Our perception of the real is mediated through representations that are constrained and within which we hypothesize about reality. The hypotheses, of course, are tied to theory. But all one can do is to hypothesize. Truth is regulative, hardly ever constitutive. As it turns out every once in a while our minds are so wired so as to posit the truth; yet this is somewhat hidden from us and rare. The adventure of inquiry, however, is not dismantled.

Thus the concept of judgment has a wide range in inquiry. The notion of a mental judgment is a deep seated one, the extension of which is varied and in some contexts chimerical. But without the notion of the mind as judgment, we would not begin to know how to understand ourselves. One can masquerade and deny its use, or think the mental eliminable, but this is wrong-headed. One should rather focus on how to make the mental as judgment more intelligible, while acknowledging the pervasiveness and primitiveness of its application.

Thoughts and Movement

We have been raised in the tradition that envisioned passion and the body as seducing the spirit. The theology was one of turning away from the illusions of the world. This was the world of "flesh and blood." Since God was "thought thinking itself," unmoved and perfect, degrees of perfection were correlated with degrees of thought (as in Aristotle). But knowledge often comes through the way the body feels the world (see chapter 8). This does not mean that thought does not mediate feelings. The body in action is embodied by mind. Mind is not thought thinking itself, but is part of the organization of our actions. The mind is active in movement. Movement is itself no privation, and thought is embodied, involving the taking in and making of a world. Since all emotions are mediated by thoughts, there is an active component. The mentation is in part tied to the conflicts of life, the dilemmas that necessitate resolution.

Summary

The main point, which has been expressed in a variety of intellectual ways in this century, is that the emotions are embedded in thoughts tied to problem solving, and making sense of things; there are no pure emotions. Inquiry helps to distill the sources of emotion and thought and helps to encourage action based on them. Inquiry helps us to arrive at sound judgments in a muddled world. Nothing is pure; expressed in the language of epistemology, certainty is rarely to be found. Pragmatism insures action; the existential part focuses on the experience.

Chapter 4

Persons in the Extreme

Introduction

What do extreme situations reveal about the nature of persons. Why do some people perish, while others cling marginally, and some even flourish? Accounts of extreme situations have tended to be used as arguments for one set of properties exclusively over other sets of properties; this may have been short sighted. Literature and life, and *pragmatic* sense, reveal that people survive in a number of ways. We need a balanced view.

This chapter begins by conveying two versions of behavior that occur in the same extreme: one results in elevating, the other in the denigration of humanness—our soul. Both are true to life. The second, third, and fourth sections are about the issues of ignorance and the victim, obedience to authority and stupidity, and the bureaucratization of assault. The fifth suggests that evil can be real, as can the hope that comes from recognizing that good does reside within people. The final section is a summary and some speculations. The important theme is that the appreciation of another's experiences can avert our more barbaric expressions and possibly, through inquiry allow civilized behavior to flourish. Inquiry includes resiliency, as well as the ability to acquire new ways of being and to imagine and execute them.

Two Accounts of Behavior in the Extreme

Terrence Des Pres argues that in extreme situations like those of a concentration camp, or a Russian Gulag, a sense of human experience emerges that is rather noble. This is one interpretation of the extreme: He likens the emergence of this experience, in its "nakedness," as a condition in which culture has been ripped from personhood. He calls such a state "Radical Nakedness." In a camp of that kind, one is given a number and one's hair and other personal expressions are taken away. One is given a uniform that is the same as everyone else's and taken to a strange place (of course this holds for recruits in the army). One is no longer a cultural being. Des Pres thinks one then stands naked. But a regrouping process emerges; survival is at stake and new roots, which are the human roots of the shared conquest of death, emerge. One possesses oneself anew, stronger than before. In Des Pres' words:[1]

> "The survivor preserves his life, but also his humanness, against a situation in which, at every turn, decency seems stupid or impossible. He anchors himself in the moral purpose of bearing witness, and thereby he maintains, in himself and in the action he performs, an integrity which contradicts the savagery surrounding him. His task is like one of those small rocks to which vast sea-plants hold upon the ocean floor—a point of stability and rooted strength against the brunt of each day's peril."

Are people really made more grand in such a place? Des Pres believes that individuals survive in such circumstances because they extend themselves to others, share common bonds and nurture one another. They perhaps are more patient and empathetic—more mature within the community and less narcissistic. In so doing, they indeed become more grand. This is a grand moment of human existence which emerges in the extreme. This conception of survival in the extreme calls to mind assertions made by sociobiologists that at the root of most animal behavior is a social bond that expresses itself in altruistic acts.[2]

There are many examples both fictional and factual to support the claims about such grand moments. Camus, for example, described the human nobility of being that emerged in a plague.[3] Because of the plague, people were pushed to the point where all things were questionable. Everything became possible because the commonplace had been shattered. In this extreme moment the noble emerged in the form of an individual who appeared as a bearer of responsibility.

In more prosaic terms, in our quotidian existence we lose access to the noble and fail to recognize what counts in life. For example, the importance of health is recognized by some by volunteering to work in a hospital. This extreme can trigger a recognition of possibilities, such as the value of one's health. One is forced into life and must take hold of it. The theologians' cry to "wake the fear of God" may be seen as a plea to awaken people from the deadness of habit. The extreme breaks the habit and we learn a lot. We experience intense emotions. People cut across color and class, and empathy and a sense of community may become more dominant. It is not the fear of God, but the awakening of life that is evoked.

People care for themselves when wounded or deprived as during a plague or in a concentration camp. We cleanse ourselves, and cleansing keeps the animal instincts alive. As Des Pres suggests,[4]

"To care for one's appearance thus becomes an act of resistance and a necessary moment in the larger structure of survival. Life itself depends on keeping dignity intact, and this, in turn, depends on the daily, never finished battle to remain visibly human."

The body is one's most intimate home. In caring for the body, a sense of embodiment occurs, a mind at home in a body (chapter 8). In times of the extreme this is called forth. We all know that the body and its care is important. The extreme awakens its recognition. The biological roots are then acknowledged and shared.

Recently, a friend's dog died. She had cancer welts in many parts of her body which she methodically licked in order to clean them. She seemed to feel better when bathed, as we would. Nurturing the body is a basic function that we use under such conditions.

Extending such care to others is also basic, because being connected is deeply important. Bodily extensions are an expression of this. There are other examples of being connected—gift-giving, for example—in which there exists a social bond.[5]

> "And like the need to bear witness, which might also be viewed rationally, there was yet an instinctive depth to the emergence of social order through help and sharing. Human interchange goes on all the time everywhere. But in the concentration camps it was more naked, more urgently pursued. Judging from the experience of survivors, "gift morality" and a will to communion are constitutive elements of humanness. In extremity, behavior of this kind emerges without plan or instruction, simply as the means to life."

And while the authorities of the camps may perceive one form of behavior—the appearance of conformity—the actual fabric of life may revolve around these other forms of behavior.[6]

> "An inmate meeting and passing an officer without causing the officer to correct the prisoner's manner appears to be an inmate properly contained in the prison and properly accepting of his imprisonment. But we know that in some cases such an inmate might be concealing under his coat a couple of bed boards to be used as roof timbers of an escape tunnel. An inmate thus equipped could stand before a prison officer and not be the person the officer was seeing, nor be in the world that the camp was supposed to impose upon him. The inmate is fixed in the camp, but his capacities have migrated. Moreover, since an overcoat can conceal clear evidence of this migration, and since a personal front involving clothing accompanies our participation in every organization, we must appreciate that any figure cut by any person may conceal evidence of spiritual leave-taking."

The extreme awakens and perhaps can also deaden. However, awakening also can occur under the less extreme, or what seems like no extreme at all. For example, gift-giving in our daily lives is exemplified when friends give each other massages to soothe their bodies.

But there is another Freudian interpretation of life in the Holocaust, which suggests that people survive in those ghastly situations because they identify with the aggressor. As a childlike egoism emerges, they take on the identity of the camp commandants. The child looks to the parent and in this case, the parents are the commanders of the prison. If people survive, they do so because they have identified with their surroundings. They lose touch with the reality of their past and their maturity, and in place of the past is the present environment. Danger is sensed. To become like the other, to blend in with the terrain and escape the danger is the desire. Having been reduced to a childlike helplessness filled with narcissistic desires, and desiring to survive at all costs, the inmate begins to support the institution and takes on the properties of the bestial. They would be closed to new experience and unable to be inquirers. In the psychoanalyst Bruno Bettelheim's words:[7]

> "The prisoners lived, like children, only in the immediate present; they lost feeling for the sequence of time; they became unable to plan for the future or to give up immediate pleasure satisfactions to gain greater ones in the near future. They were able to establish durable object-relations. Friendships developed as quickly as they broke up. Prisoners would, like early adolescents, fight one another tooth and nail, declare that they would never again look at one another or speak to one another, and become close friends once more within a few minutes. They were boastful, telling tales about what they had accomplished in their former lives, or how they succeeded in cheating foremen or guards, and how they sabotaged the work. Like children, they felt not at all set back or ashamed when it became known that they had lied about their prowess."

Bettelheim spent time in a concentration camp. Vivid depictions of such surviving can also be found in other places too. The phenomenon is real and one can imagine surviving that way as well. Many of us would—too many.

However, one can also imagine surviving by being noble and resisting the savagery and the identity of the commandants. But the moral is that people survive in both manners. To deny either is foolish. Is one more dominant than the other? It is hard to say. Moreover, many people are all too human and break down from the effects of such an extreme instance. Their bodies are just too frail. They may rise to the moment, but fall. Some do not rise at all. Much depends on the person, and the circumstances. One would hope to be noble, but one might be base or just human, and bits of both.

Ignorance and the Victim

Hannah Arendt suggests that some of the fault for the Holocaust lay with the victims themselves.[8] She claims that the Jews' naiveté in politics and their unwillingness to be public contributed significantly to their destruction. This blindness had both a political and social price, and because Arendt felt that they were culpable in part for their own genocide, she caused a great stir in the Jewish community.

There may have been ignorance on the part of the Jews; there was human frailty. But to acknowledge such frailty is to begin to assume responsibility in the face of what is being presented. No doubt many refused to acknowledge what might happen and was happening. This has been a common theme in many of the discussions of the victims of the Holocaust—any Holocaust. Not wanting to believe, remaining private, is a deep-seated feature of people. People often stand ignorant, in part, because of "bad faith." A childlike defiance emerges and the mythical denial of painful reality is made manifest. This is the childlike regression, or fixation, talked about.

Children and idiots, often private, retreat in the face of reality (chapter 5). Maturity and publicity are connected: therein lies responsibility. The concept of being public is elevated to a great height for Arendt. Not being public makes one prone to idiocy. To the extent to which the Jews fell short of political consciousness instantiated in public stances,

Arendt passes the judgment of culpability. Even though this privacy is a mark of immaturity and it expresses the desire to avoid what is being presented, culpability or responsibility holds.

For Arendt the denial of reality is mainly a matter of human ignorance and stupidity, and not the added property of being a child or a matter of being simply human. People just do not know any better; Arendt asserts that they should have, as if it is mainly a matter of knowledge. It is not, and Arendt's analysis is written in retrospect.

Who really believed at the time that such acts could occur? Many Jewish leaders thought it best to try to work with the Nazis, to save their communities. This was not such a cowardly or ignorant thing to do.[9] Often what outwardly appears like conformity is in reality not so. Pacts among individuals are held and the outward appearances are intentionally deceptive as was already indicated and well known. Finally, some people labored to save, and many could see the possibility of some hope, so they followed along.

Arendt also forgets that the Jews were not allowed a forum in which to be public, from without as well as from within their communities. Neither is it just a matter of ignorance or privacy—the lack of a public stance—that led the Jews astray, nor is it weakness or blind obedience. None of these explanations is entirely explanatory of the phenomenon, but each captures a partial truth. We just do not know the values of these variables. Some people were ignorant, others weak, others childlike; some bestial, some heroic. In each we attribute responsibility to varying degrees, for which most fall short.

Having mentioned the victims, consider the oppressors and their denial of responsibility.

Obedience and Stupidity

The experiments of Stanley Milgram are instructive with regard to the issue of blind obedience, or the behavior of Nazi guards.[10] While Arendt was commenting on the Eichmann trial, Milgram was studying the behavior of people in laboratories. His experiments were designed to say something about how people respond to authority, even if the orders are barbaric. He made people administer electric shocks to other people because they were told to. The shocks were actually fake, but the people giving them did not know this. Had the shocks been real, they would have caused a lot of pain; they might even have killed someone. The participants heard fake screams from the persons they thought were receiving the shock, yet they continued to administer the shocks. When asked later why, they said that they were just following orders. The moral is that the Nazi and the person next door converge; both could hurt you. They attribute the responsibility to an authority that is parental in scope; the follower childlike in obedience. The result is a base human expression.

Eichmann has been described as a bureaucrat, a small minded person no different from many of us; "this man was not a monster."[11] His evil was banal, or nonexistent. The man was not evil, just stupid or without class, bound by authority with little thought. He may be described as an authoritarian personality—rigidly bound by rules.[12] He did what he was told. As Arendt remarks ". . . he never harbored any ill feelings against his victims."[13] How much can we hold such people responsible? We hold them very responsible out of necessity for social order and ontic commitment to human life and its preservation and cultivation.

The Nazis often said that they were just following orders. They compartmentalized the brutality of their job from the rest of their life; they were often loving husbands.[14] They failed to appreciate the experiences of others, the result of which, as suggested in the first chapter, is barbaric and myopic behavior and impoverished perspectives on the world. They failed to recognize the suffering of others.[15]

A blind obedience to the social order was enlisted. Eichmann said repeatedly that he was following orders, as did many others, and that is what many of us say when we are told we have done something wrong. We say "we were just following so and so. I did not realize what I was doing; I didn't consider the implications." This last excuse raises the issue of ignorance. This ignorance is often self-imposed, or in bad faith. Trying to find the person who made the decision to take responsibility is a difficult chore. Perhaps inquiry and responsibility are interdependent. An inquirer must seek out what are his domains of responsibility. To be responsible means to test situations and say can I do more or better in this area?

The Milgram experiments showed that the person next door is likely to behave in a Nazi-like way under some conditions, and the Arendt account of Eichmann parallels Milgram's findings. In both cases this barbaric behavior is explained as blind obedience. They do not inquire. As Milgram puts it:[16]

> "...the most fundamental lesson of our study: ordinary people, simply doing their jobs, and without any particular hostility on their part, can become agents in a terrible destructive process. Moreover, even when the destructive effects of their work become patently clear, and they are asked to carry out actions incompatable with fundamental standards of morality, relatively few people have the resources needed to resist authority. A variety of inhibitions against disobeying authority come into play and successfully keep the person in his place."

But did Milgram's subjects ever enjoy administering the shock? When Milgram asked his subjects how they felt, they often said that they hated doing what they were doing. And the closer in distance the "shocker" was to the "sufferer," the more trouble they had. The same holds in war.[17] The further away the enemy is, the easier it is to destroy him. The closer and the more human their features become, the more difficult it is to act. We all know this phenomenon. In Milgram's terms, if the scream was far away, it was easier to shock, if the scream was close, it was far more difficult.

But there was no evidence that the subjects enjoyed causing the pain. They complained bitterly that they wanted to stop, that the punishment was inhumane, yet they continued. They knew better, but they complied.

Some Nazi bureaucrats also said they did not enjoy the chores. This is more difficult to believe. In wartime the enemy is evil and brutality is justified. This is closer to the Nazi. In the words of J. Glen Gray:[18]

> "Today I yelled at a character who had lied to me and took a certain pleasure in seeing the perspiration come to his face and his hands tremble. He knew the power I had over him. So do one's values become corrupted and conscience coarsened by the ordeal."

A fraternal bond of belonging to the group over and against another group takes hold. The psychology is us against them—clan psychology. Again, in Gray's words:[19]

> "The secret of comradeship has not been exhausted however, in the feeling of freedom and power instilled in us by communal effort in combat. There is something more and equally important. The sense of power and liberation that comes over men at such moments stems from a source beyond the union of men."

They stand fraternally connected with their comrades, motivated into action. The enemy is dehumanized while the other becomes truly "other." Their experience is denied.

Finally, it should be noted that it was Arendt, and not Milgram, who pushed the point of ignorance. Arendt probably believed, in the spirit of Augustine, that people could not be said to know and still act so bestial; they must be ignorant. In essence this is her depiction of Eichmann. By contrast, one might say that Milgram highlights another issue—weakness of will and the power of bureaucratic authority. Milgram's subjects thought that they were causing pain, yet they continued. They were not ignorant people; it was, in part, weakness of will.

Habits and Bureaucracy

Why did the Nazis continue to exterminate human life when they knew the war would be over soon and they had lost and might be held accountable for their crimes? They acted as if their appetites were deadlocked, and the need to take life were insatiable. Instead of two bodies provoking satiety, 10 did, then 100, then 1000. Then none did. It was an addiction. Their will was fixated (chapter 5); they continued to kill.

Some Nazis thought that they were doing the world a favor because the indictment against the Jews seemed warranted to them. Moreover, an implicit acceptance of such acts may have been sustained, since the Allies certainly knew of the camps and did nothing to stop the extermination.[20] Some people caught in the web of bureaucracy were probably trying just to finish the job they had begun. Once one is caught in a bureaucratic trap, finishing a job at all begins to seem virtuous.[21] Perhaps this is the thoughtless part, or the disintegrated self. What one might have been reluctant to do in the beginning will be accomplished in the end. Habits set in. Neither Jews nor others were killed in great numbers for many years, but then were slaughtered desperately when the Nazis were already losing the war. The machine had a life of its own, and once set in motion it took over. What may have happened was a fixation of habit that grew more intense as time went by. In the end, there was not much of a person left. There was little freedom or choice; the habit raped the will. There was no mature responsible agent.

The slaughter disgusts. The Milgram experiments remind us of what we can do to each other. A glance at a history book is also a reminder. One needs these pedagogic reminders to protect ourselves. We basically know it and yet we need to be told, called upon, awakened, educated, and reminded. And yet, that probably still is not enough.

Thus, the psychology of bestiality emerges in the habits of the small at an extreme time. People on either side do not become noble in the extreme. The horror may begin moderately, and end quite differently. To keep the habit alive, the intensity increases; so then does the destruction. To keep the habit alive the stimulation must increase. Obedience is the constant call and the flock follows in a masquerade of excuses.

The immature, the idiot, and the dangerous become embodied in one form.

Evil

In dark times, enmeshed in a culture that blinds and produces an ethic of vulgarity, the systematic brutality of a people is made actual. Many of the people who do the brutalizing follow orders, some are not intelligent, and most pretend not to know; some probably enjoy it. The acts are nonetheless horrible, whatever the reasons. This fact can never be denied.

On occasion people do enjoy causing pain while they are cognizant of their actions. This is evil. Most contemporary accounts of bestial behavior render such acts human and normal, thus making their accounts so shocking. It has often been claimed,[22] that Nazis did not enjoy the chore. However, under some conditions people do inflict pain on others and know they are doing wrong. Some of the Nazis, perhaps a lot of them, may have in fact enjoyed their activities, which included inflicting pain. This was in the face of knowledge of their actions, not just innocence, stupidity, bureaucratic entrapment, or weakness of will. It is evil simply when one knows better and yet chooses, and to some extent enjoys an act of bestial behavior.

The Nazis, and any kindred kind, can kill so methodically because the victim was not considered a full person. The person was no longer human. This is analogous to the Milgram experiments where the scream is less human because it is far away. The destruction is inflicted with less conflict, since dehumanization makes it is easy to kill.

Self-imposed ignorance reduces whatever conflict the individual might experience. We all do it to varying degrees when we look away from the sufferings of people and animals around us. We fail to acknowledge their *experience*; we fail to behave rationally. The Nazis did it to an extreme. Nothing sublime is awakened; only a deadly habit is formed—murdering. There are many extremes that provoke nothing noble once the deadness of the fixation of belief has settled in. Once this fixation takes over, the robbery of sentience makes the endeavor of destruction easier. If one hears the discomfort it is a lot harder to hurt the person. Therefore, keeping them away and stripping them of their personhood will make it that much easier to hurt them. Habits and the rape of the will grow in strength and block the expression of the noble in the extreme.

Conclusion: Surviving the Experience

The extreme demands action in response. It can produce noble or pathologic behavior. The therapist speaks of how such extremes cripple people by radically undermining the very fabric of their lives. Having survived in any manner, one's well being is severely hampered from then on. Also, many survive in the extreme not because they become particularly good or bad, but because they are very cunning. They get close to the right people and act as they need to in order to make it. They survive. Survival at times requires the dissolution of the grand self, of the hero who rises to the occasion in outspoken exuberance. In fact, a "minimal self" is how one may survive—no heroism, no grandeur, just survival.[23]

But one is reminded of some great acts. One of them is the grand Doctor of Orphans.[24] He cared for the children of the Warsaw Ghetto. In the end he led the children in song when they were ordered to die. He chose to die with them. It was a moment of extreme that manifested the noble. Without that voice there is no hope.

There are others who have personified the noble. One notable person is the Swedish diplomat Raoul Wallenburg, who gave up his freedom and probably his life to save Hungarian Jews during the war.

But most people just follow, their nobility never awakened. The whole event is an eternal bad dream. There are many other examples of barbaric behavior.

The debate between the bestial and small, and the gallant and large is embedded in a philosophical tradition that tries to capture what is at the heart of human experience. Where Hobbes railed that life "was nasty, brutish and short" and thought it was best to keep persons away from one another lest they hurt each other, he expressed a dim view of human nature.[25] By contrast Rousseau believed that persons embody a beautiful state of grace when left to their natural ways.[26] He seemed to think that there is peace and good living when cultural influences are eliminated. These two themes regarding the nature of people are captured in the accounts given by Bettelheim and Des Pres with regard to surviving in the concentration camp. Both presuppose psychological conceptions of human nature. Bettelheim is immersed in the psychoanalytic tradition and Des Pres, in grand humanistic expressions such as can be found in the works of Camus. The first is more closely related to Hobbes, the second to Rousseau.

Pedagogy and inquiry are the major hope for humanity. This is naive, but it is not absurd. We need the creative moral use of mind in curbing destructive tendencies, thereby helping to insure civility. In overcoming idiocy, or immaturity, we are shoved into the public, and a shared responsibility among individuals may emerge. The extreme can elevate it into fact, or denegrate it into a myth. Our nature embodies both the bestial and the grand. Pedagogy reminds us that "Never shall I forget these things, even if I am condemned to live as long as God Himself. Never."[27]

Still, one does not have to be in such extreme situations to appreciate the sense of survival. Ordinary life teaches one the lesson of survival, and it is in the face of this that inquiry becomes essential.

Chapter 5

Madness and the Soul

Introduction

James, of all the pragmatists, addressed issues of madness and models of sanity. He had met Freud when Freud came to America, and no doubt would have been influenced by him, if James had lived longer.

This chapter is thus about two mental factors: the self and the will. Developmental, psychoanalytic, cognitive, and biological issues figure heavily in the discussion. The thread is naturalistic. For the soul to reach its fullest expression there must be an integration of the mature self and the healthy will. A developed and mature self is tied to others via human bonds. The will requires discipline through its exercise in action; that is, the will disciplines and becomes healthy as it is exercised in its approach and avoidance of events. Integration of the self and the will is important for the soul, the best expression of our humanity (as in Aristotle, Nichomachean Ethics).

In modern terms, the self captures something of what we mean by the subjective and the objective.[1] We are the subjects having the experiences (chapter 1), looking out on the world, performing acts. While there is no core self, self expression is tied to our sense of freedom and dignity.

The self and the expression of freedom are to some extent demonstrated through self control. Thus throughout life both the will and the self are intimately connected to our sense of freedom. Aberrations in the development of self lead to madness and psychosis. Aberrations of the will can lead to

69

addictions and dependencies. In the absence of the sense of self, or of the will, madness and addiction prevail.

Such dependencies and addictions, madness and fragmentation, reflect a phenomenon of stagnation, of being frozen or entrapped. The result is the loss of freedom, and what freedom there is is limited. That is, the freedom is within constraints and is tied to the integration of the developed non-narcissistic self and the exercised and directed will. The sad fact of humanity is the existence of the fragmented self and the misdirected will, which can lead to being frozen.

Though the self and the will overlap, they are not metaphysical substances, but are products of the brain and social constructions. Our common discourse presents many points where they functionally overlap—where the pathology of one has consequences for the other.

The self appears to be more closely related to content and structure, the will with the discipline to carry out things. One model of this integration of the self and the will is the "spiritual warrior."[2] The content of the mature self needs valor to carry it foward in the face of the difficulties of life. This is the will.

A sense of stoicism is therefore recommended for living the good life, because deterministic factors are powerful. Our recourse in life is that the developed self and the exercised will are how we take hold of our lives through self-determination, leading to an obvious moral imperative, namely, that a sense of empathy for ourselves and others, who are frozen, is essential. Perhaps inquiry is vital to building a healthy self.

Healthy Development of the Self

Mahler has characterized the development of the self and the importance of object relations, the relations to others with a sense of the world.[3] Her theory is that aberrations of the self emerge when the child's actions are not mirrored by a kindly adult, or when a healthy symbiosis is not achieved. The child is able to move outside herself by seeing her reflection in the friendly eye of another, e.g., the parent. There is a kinesthetic antecedent to this. The child moves through the world, occasionally glancing back for reassurance, and then she continues. This enables her to learn about her strengths and weaknesses. The key for the parent in this situation is to lend support without smothering the child.[4] Development proceeds from a oneness with the mother or primary caretaker, to the fear of alienation and separation from her, to acceptance and a sense of solidarity with the world. The body, which Freud likens to the basic sense of self, figures importantly in the first flight of independence (chapter 8). The development of motor control plays a role in the child's development of individuation and prowess—in being able to move around, explore, and master the world.

The child learns about transition through objects that come and go and their interactions with these objects.[5] They expend effort; the first sense of the will and the emergence of the feeling of efficacy.[6] Their sense of self increases as the world becomes more familar. Their prowess as an individual is beginning to be felt. They develop good ego defenses, which become a part of their organized personality. They learn to recognize others, and move away from narcissistic demands of immediate pleasures and control of others. They develop some maturity, becoming their own person—their own self, and learn self-mastery. A sense of play and mastery come into prominence. Through inquiry the children learn about what is and what is not themselves; the link between exploring and playing. Play may lend itself to inquiry and mastery. A self in relation to the world has overcome, to some extent, infantile egoism. There is a new sense of oneness and separateness with the world, as well as togetherness with it. A sense of well-being and the capacity for maintainence of self-esteem emerges.

Dewey's emphasis on *transactions* was to highlight what happens everyday;[7] transactional engagements are expressed in the daily life of being with others, recognizing, and engaging them. A respect for the being of others emerges from being connected to them; one senses their life and their experience as being different from one's own. One tends to minimize the damage one does to others, by being cognizant of the other (chapter 1). The intrusion is minimized and a greater sense of relatedness develops. There is respect and greater freedom, and sense of responsibility appears. This power of self-actualization is a dynamic event with real possibilities for expressing one's prowess—all one can be.

The Western tradition has stated that maturity is related to the development of freedom and autonomy,[8] and choice is a direct expression of the self and contributes to its development. This development of the self is an achievement. It requires the recognition of others, or what James or Mead and others called the social or spiritual self.[9] A sense of humor, irony, and perhaps emphathy are necessary.[10]

Self-preservation is another factor for the healthy self and is tied to our happiness. Our desire to survive is biologically based. Living things struggle to continue and proliferate, a basic need for self-preservation. Self control is the key to our liberation and is tied to our development. We learn to control our behavior and to avoid harmful things. In self mastery there is dissolution of extraneous desires and the mastery of infant cravings. In this case, there is a transcendence of frozen infantile desires of the self.[11]

Failure to Develop a Healthy Self

Aberrations of an autonomous sense of self emerge when the process of normal psychological development breaks down. There is a lack of effective *inquiry*; the world is shut down. One result is that dependencies and weaknesses of will can become rampant. The separation of parent and child can be like withdrawal from a drug. We cling to the mother of infant fantasy; it provides us with a sense of euphoria and narcosis. In separating away from the mother we fear the total loss of her. If the mother, or parent, is not perceived as good the child often develops poorly.[12] Good mothering is defined by healthy contact and good results. A sense of being related to others emerges. In the biologically sound child this object relatedness helps protect against pathologies. Without it solipsism is the result and idiocy is the expression. A look into the world is lost. By idiocy I mean loss of the world, a result of being lost in one's world; others fall out of sight.

Excessive dependency is one type of developmental pathology. "Magical" thinking is one outcome of such dependency. The recognition of reality and responsiveness to it are thwarted. The private inner world of fantasy develops instead, and remains tied to inaction. The world is lost. The self either fails to develop, decomposes, or develops into an unstable self. A pathological desire to control others takes precedence. Extreme pathologies, such as autism, psychosis, and schizophrenia may emerge.

The trauma of early life fragment the development of the self into the good self and bad self, the good object and the bad object, or the good and bad breast.[13] Cognitive dissonance emerges with splitting as the possible result. The real becomes blurred. A sense of persecution results in a lack of integration and good judgment. The world is depersonalized and one is divorced from it. On the other hand, it may be overpersonalized by one's projections. The individual remains at the level of identification with, rather than developing a sense of separateness in relation to others.

Attachment to others is essential for development; the development of the self, and the sense of object relatedness depends on it. The capacity to grow beyond the exclusivity of the good and the bad as the basic cognitive-emotional evaluation, to avoid splitting where the good and bad objects become mutually inaccessible to one another depends on connectedness to others. This leads to greater integration. Without this evolving integration of the self, projection can become a dominant defense. The harm that one does to oneself is attributed to the world. The world is bad, not the self. Denial is met at every corner.

Borderline patients have unstable ego boundaries, and object-relatedness is blurred.[14] One part of this pathology is something akin to the child with transitional objects.[15] The pathology blurs the distinction between self and other. Others are at the border of being real and not real, there and not there. Some remain at this phase in development, which may lead to the emergence of the angry child.[16]

The child feels abused and becomes enraged, but its rage is denied. The parents deny it, making it difficult for the child to accept it. The child represses it, splitting it off from consciousness. The good and bad selves are further splintered. Rage lurks both underneath and at the surface, and masks feelings of helplessness. The divided remains of a splintered self dominates and pervades most impressions. The rage of helplessness predominates and expresses itself through constant projection of itself onto others. There may also be a continual attempt to escape from the old traumatized self: a desire to shift away from the real internal conflict. The event is violently repressed and the rage is deep, resulting in the appearance of a maddened self, a dissolved self. Self-aggrandizement is one compensation for such dissolution.

Narcissism is in fact a loss of "selfhood"[17] and blinds the capacity for inquiry. Narcissistic people do not relate properly to others; solipsism is one result, psychosis or madness another. This leads to narcissistic emptiness in life, dulls the pre-occupation with the self. The narcissist is prone to addiction, excessive dependencies, and reliance on others to build self-esteem. Everything comes from without, little from within.

The Will

Pragmatists emphasize effort, or the will.[18] And the self and the will are intimately connected. Through willed actions the person establishes continuity. Without this ability life falters, like a dying limb on a tree, withering away. Creation of self depends upon willed actions.[19] That is, the will is presupposed in self-creation because struggle and strife are usually involved.

German philosophers in particular emphasize the will. For some thinkers we are what we will, and the self is the primeval will or a "will to power."[20] In this sense, the will is tied to an affirmation of being, individuality, and the expression of power—an ever expanding expression of the self.

The will is related to a basic sense of self, and the actualization of the self is tied to the expression of the will.

The will lends decisiveness and gives the ability to carry out decisions. When will is lost a schizophrenic experience may appear, as if something takes over.

Importantly, the will gives meaning to life, and is an expression of the desire to live, the move away from despondency and helplessness. This move is tied to self-determination. The will is related to purpose and attention is important for carrying out ideas, and in controlling intellect, e.g., perception, learning, and memory. The will is evoked in changing habits, in overcoming obstacles, in reaching goals. It is therefore tied to the good, and the avoidance of harmful things that restrict our sense of freedom. The will is therefore also essential for survival. In addition, it is causative. These facts highlight the relationship between purpose, the self and the fact that the will is essential for morality.[21]

The great Greek triad (Socrates, Plato, Aristotle) taught that the will needs guidance, that it is tied to reason and gives meaning to events. If divorced from reason, it can become barbaric. A delicate balance exists between reason and the will. When the will is only permitted to strive blindly it becomes destructive. If it is overloaded with reason it becomes impotent and fragmented. Fragmentation leads to weakness of the will. In the weak, unguided will, impulsive, compulsive, and obsessive behaviors are apparent. The sense of purpose that emerges from the self, and that rules our lives to some extent, has to be clear; otherwise, the will splinters and disintegrates. On the other hand, one can have a clear sense of purpose but still be stuck. This is sometimes expressed as stubbornness. Stubbornness is also tied to too much willfulness.

Weakness of will can be manifest in the tendency to give in to authorities, to follow orders thoughtlessly, to give into our desires to be controlled, and to lose individuality. The will is important in standing up to the world, and to ourselves. The will is essential in the realization of the self; it is the vehicle that preserves the self. It is important in that it helps to resist social political structures and dead or bad habits. Addictions and other afflictions rape the will, and a weak will leads to addictions. Escape is one motive for the addict: narcosis the desire, narcotics the answer.

Freedom of the will is an integration of one's desires guided by a healthy self. But many times no matter how much one wants to change, or will something, we cannot do it; there are things outside of our will.[22] The answer to what they are is often unclear.

Regression as Advancement

In neurological terms we speak of the "dissolution" of brain and behavior (see chapter 9), as the reverse of evolution, or a return to the more primitive. This occurs when the brain is damaged—typically the cortex. The cortex is the more evolved brain tissue, and therefore one is forced to rely on the more primitive brain tissue when it is damaged. Regressions are also a return to the primitive. If by analogy the cortex and its use are like maturing and evolving during development, then regression is like moving out of the neocortex and back into the limbic system or brainstem to the older parts of the brain. The developed self can come into contact with its repressed primitive precursor.

This regression of the self can be a constructive advancement. After such a regression the subject's focus can still be present (chapter 1). This willful dissolution of self can lead to generosity and communion with others. The importance of others is recognized; we are all part of the same adventure. Such regressions have the air of play and are tied to our capacity to muse about the world and ourselves, to engage the world, and to learn from it. A sense of civility is tied to this sort of dissolution. A community emerges to celebrate an adventure; we take part in the festival. The fantasy of a fragile but real democratic harmony of action may result.

The mature self thus seeks eros or communion with others. The dissolution of the self is related to things larger than the self, which leads to fraternity with others. The emptying of one's individual concerns is a prerequisite. The emptiness is not necessarily a negative one. Dissolution of the self leads to the emergence of a new being or self. This is essential for liberation and peace. It is the drive for eros or love that leads to the completion of our being.

Fixation and Change

When fixated inappropiately, pathos continues to control the individual. Such people appear stuck or trapped in a fixation of belief. Events and experiences of childhood, those binding factors on the brain (chapter 9), lead to entrapment which often emerges in adulthood, and which may also result from adult experiences. Beliefs are fixated, as is the resolve of the will.

Therapy offers some prospect of recovery and dissolving "bad bonds" to "bad objects,"[23] possibly leading to the development of healthier relationships. Therapy provides a means for regression, or returning to the early developmental aberration of the self and its relationship to the world by engaging narcissistic dependencies directly.[24] One reason for the return is the desire for union and symbiosis with the distant past. The world is a terrifying place in which one fends for oneself. There are dangers. Escape from the loss of the world means the loss of the dangers; the idea of the return is peaceful.

The therapeutic hope is to uncover, and then move away from this state, to change one's sense of self-esteem. But at times the "analyzed becomes addicted to the analyst."[25] The self remains fragmented; freedom is far off. It has been suggested that normal neurosis is the best one can expect from therapy.[26] In development, one goes from the paranoid-schizoid state to a depressed and more realistic state, that is, from the unrealistic to the realistic.[27] In therapy, one moves from delusional to real depression (depression with good reason, given the nature of the world and the self).

This view is too bleak. As a pragmatist, I believe there is the possibility that change can occur, with a much more positive sense to it. Thus although a person may be at the edge of life, in the chaos of the splintered and beleagured self and will, there may be a moment of self-affirmation. Partial unity surfaces in the face of splintering, but it may require faith, courage and as James understood a "will to believe" to persevere.[28] Self-affirmation begins, possibly without normal depression or neurosis.

Freedom and Necessity

The self and the will are instantiated by the brain. We believe this because aberrations of the will emerge when the brain is damaged, e.g., in victims of Parkinson's disease, obsessive-compulsives, or perhaps in addicts. In these cases the expression of the will is outside of one's control. Pathologies of the brain also break the structure, cohesiveness, and content of the self.

Sometimes our choices determine us, and we become stuck with what we choose (see chapter 10). We know that biological and genetic factors help determine who we are, but do not know to what extent. We believe that experiential events during critical periods of development as well as conditioning factors help to determine us.[29]

What freedom do we have then? Freedom has often been thought as being in one's nature (Augustine), or better expressed as fullfilling or "actualizing" one's nature. As the Shaker song expresses it, it is "a gift to find out where one ought to be"—to be in the right place and to become more of what one is is, that is, if you are lucky and have something to look foward to. If not, you are in trouble—the common trauma of humanity.

In addition, there is a tendency to remain in something despite the fact that it is harmful. The silent, and not so silent, sad cries of being imprisoned are heard everywhere. The constraining factors of the ontogenetic and phylogenetic past are great determining factors. At times we choose our constraints; we narrow our choices (chapter 10). Therefore, we can only strive for limited freedom amidst some great moments of expression.

This limited freedom has its roots in evolution. With greater unity and adaptability there is a wider range of niches one can respond to and live in, and therefore, greater choices (chapter 10). The evolution of the self and the will that distinguishes us from other animals involves the capacity to change, our recognition of a greater power outside of ourselves, and the desire to be different.[30] Those with limited freedom want what they want. Those in the bondage of addictions struggle with the inconsistencies of their wants, since many addicts have desires of not being addicted. They are splintered, divided, and at times deceitful.

There is change, but it is limited and partial. There are moments when one takes a leap of faith, and change is abrupt. "But all things excellent are as difficult as they are rare."[31]

The Soul

For Aristotle an important concern in the causation of animal life is the soul, and gives life to bodies. But the soul is not incorporeal as argued by Aquinas. The highest soul, asserted Aristotle, can exist without a body. For pragmatists the soul has to be corporal to have life. The full expression of self and will is the humanity that lies in our souls. This is the Aristotelian sense—self-actualization. There is also the Platonic sense of becoming more than the acknowledged potential by taking in new things.

The expression of the soul is a life project. Perhaps this is part of what one means by spiritual inquiry. The sense of connectedness with others in a community is a fundamental constituent in the soul's fullfillment. The important point is that we live with our souls.[32] Acceptance eases the soul, but it is also the soul that grieves and bares the pain of our condition.

The soul enjoys its own company, solitude, and aloneness along with the connectedness to others on its journey toward enlightenment's deep perspectives on the world and the recognition of the ephemeral and the worthy. Through this adventure the soul comes to expression by the development of insight, inquiry, and self-control.

Chapter 6

Leadership and Inquiry

Introduction: Beliefs and Doubt

Our beliefs are our guides; they form the habits that orchestrate our actions. Without beliefs we could not get about. We usually do not purposefully challenge our beliefs, they are challenged from without, and when they break down we grudgingly search for new ones. This produces discomfort of not knowing what to do and how to act.

We desire and pursue steady states, a basic feature of animal life. Human knowers desire stability and regulation. When an expectation is broken, the inquirer (like most humans and other animals) is left uncomfortable. The breakdown causes an itch that cannot quite be scratched, because there is no knowledge of how to do it. At first there is denial. Before acknowledging the new itch the inquirer tenaciously holds onto the old beliefs, but finally he acquiesces and confronts the problem. Such was Peirce's description of belief and action.[1]

Inquirers and the Community: An Overview

There was a sense among philosophers of science in the first half of this century that scientists were different from the rest of us; they were considered more rational. In the last part of this century we have become wiser. Inquirers are human and subject to many of the same ills as the rest of humanity. Scientific inquiry is now rarely performed in the same manner by the adventuring mind as it was in the past (e.g., Galileo), and has now become industrialized; being in a laboratory is being part of a large staff. The workers on the staff are modular and work is highly specialized. There is also another factor at work—the desire not to have to think independently. These factors limit the capacity to think creatively, to challenge, and to engage.

There is an old and important point, that inquiry and inquirers are identified with liberation (e.g., Bacon). The human presence at such times is elevated. The world's salvation is achieved, in part, through the quest and attainment of knowledge. Dewey stated in numerous places that this pedagogical adventure is therefore tied to democracy and civilization.[2]

Knowledge can be power, and power can be abusive, especially when it is only internal—that is, when there are no external constraints on its use (or when it is tied to an overzealous sense of objectivity). That is why civil governments divide power. The power is then not internal to one body, but distributed across several bodies with checks and balances.

As frameworks that guide inquiry become entrenched, they attain power. The every-day inquirer becomes institutionalized by the framework. Habits of action are established that define the inquiry. Those who resist the institutional framework for inquiry may be abused, because dissent is not appreciated. It is a social psychological fact that we do not tolerate dissent very well. This is a common theme in human life.

Unfortunately, humans tend to get lost in the bureaucratic institutional setting. The individual falters and withers away; inquiry fades. The omnipresent institution often promotes thoughtless bureaucracies. Thoughtless action happens in inquiry as elsewhere, in part because frameworks are tenaciously held by people, often with great subtlety and self deception.

Communities and Inquirers

Classical pragmatists acknowledged an obvious truth, that we can not exist without a public. We are tied to communities (chapter 2). Only idiots are without a public forum. But while we exist within institutional public places, we stand apart from the institution while nurturing both it and ourselves. We are aligned to the public, or the community, but are critical of it. This is not an easy position in which to be and there is no magic cure in rationality, no authority to obscure the issues. The inherent conflict is real, not imagined. The individual stands alone as a mind, and yet is tied to an imperfect public. The individual is public—related, connected, supportive, and critical.

We find cultural evolution in many practices in the diverse communities of garment workers or laboratory scientists. Traditions that organize action are handed down from generation to generation. In both communities knowledge is accumulated of how to do and understand things. In both communities people often cling to what works and resist change until there is little choice. Action is guided, beliefs are applied and defended, behavior is organized. In both communities, the drive to create is strong for some who come forward with new ideas. The institution may then shake or topple.

But despite the commonalities in the two communities, there is a profound commitment to the growth of knowledge in laboratory science where inquiry and the search for truth are in some real sense the dominant concerns. This is not true of the garment community. That knowledge means significantly more for the community of inquirers cannot be denied. Consider the implications for humanity of the recent finding that transplants of fetal brain tissue into the brains of Parkinson's patients corrects some of their motor abnormalities. Such examples convince us that there is real growth in knowledge.

The knowledge acquired in the community of scientific inquirers is more valued than that in the community of garment workers. We value highly the knowledge that helps reduce illness, organizes just political practices, or fosters self-awareness. This is prized knowledge, more valued than the knowledge of which slacks are in style and how to top the next market. Despite our daily behavior, we know what is of value, and at choice moments many of us demonstrate that knowledge.

But despite these facts about the growth and value of knowledge, most inquirers resist the acceptance of new beliefs, remain tied to old ones, and are forced to think openly only when their beliefs break down. Nonetheless, it is through "normal science" of the day to day "miniscus" readings where a lot of the work is accomplished.[3] Despite the fact that many people are simply being led, they are still essential ingredients in the progress of science. There are many significant technical details to labor over, an important part of science. The good part of specialization is the degree to which we have greater detail of individual systems.

It is also important to note that inquirers, like others, are often guided by charismatic figures to whose prowess they submit.[4] Inquirers do what they are told; they do what needs to be done. The leader often decides about the research and areas to inquire into and the tools to use. The rest follow with mild discontent. Despite this, there is at times, to some extent, an aura of discontent that can generate an advance in the growth of knowledge but can also demoralize as the limitations of the leader and the research viewpoints become evident.

In each generation new people emerge, few of whom are inquirers to any great extent. The motive for truth, as Whitehead suggested, is a faint one.[5] But some come to challenge the authority of the leader and the conventions. Their motives are mixed and include self-aggrandizement, the desire for perfection and the delight of truth. New methods and new ways of looking at things are proposed. A new "smell" now permeates and replaces the old one. The old investigations wither; rebellious investigators are removed. The majority convert, made too uncomfortable if they do not. The dominant ones consolidate power, establish councils, and delegate authority to chosen people. The process solidifies, beliefs take hold, conventions are institutionalized and the flock follows. Of the majority in the new framework, many are mildly in discomfort but do not deny and resist the rest.

But there is no reason to despair. All is not that bad— leaders and frameworks come and go. Knowledge, however,

seems to accrue and the discovery of truth, though frail, continues. Still many of the debates in the institution of inquiry become all too academic, often taking place in a vacuum. They are often forgotten, unless the fights are bloody, if some basic truth emerges, or if it is a worthy scandal. Mostly, they are forgotten. Miraculously, some people are genuinely able to sustain the ideals of inquiry with its beauty and the growth of knowledge that results.

Hiding

People often want success and safety. The same holds for those who do research. They often jump on the current bandwagon. In inquiry, this orientation sometimes works. As mentioned, normal science carries much of the weight of inquiry. There is nothing embarrassing about this property of our nature. Some people in the community follow the dominant person, or view, to a greater degree. We are all condemned to follow it a bit. What warrants embarrassment is that often there is not a lot of thought involved. In fact, often most people go out of their way not to think or to escape from freedom.[6] Inquiry is then blind—myopic—the labor ill spent. Also, many are just trying to move ahead. The worker bees want to make it. They want success in the community; a good living, some status, respect. And why not? The desire for success and safety is a legitimate motive.

But there is something called "secondness." The term was invented by Peirce to depict the resistance of the world to our actions. The world says "that's not the way it is" to some hypotheses. It is what laboratory scientisists call the shock of data. Therefore, because there is a limit to denial of the institutionalization of false beliefs, inquiry is different from other human events. Truth, the ideal of inquiry, does emerge. The individual knows this at some level. Some act on it, others harbor its value implicitly.

The moral is that inquiry should not be denigrated. We need to face more squarely that inquirers are neither God-like nor Satanic. While the natural desire to know, a lively sentiment, leads people into inquiry in the first place, it is all too easily thwarted. Inquiry requires cultivation, as does our protection against thoughtlessnes.

Education

Part of the social psychology of inquiry is to avoid irritable contrary data. Inquiry is hard work, and it is uncomfortable to confront the contrary. The mind is at ease or asleep when living in a narcosis or an opiated state. There are no itches to scratch, no discomforts, no need to search for new hypotheses or solve novel problems. One seeks to sleep through the life of the mind, acquiring and maintaining the deadness of habit, the blind conformity of our entrenched beliefs that regulate and guide inquiry as thoughtless institutionalized actions.

Consider professors who come to realize the perils of inquiry. Some look to hide. Disillusionment, then demoralization occurs for some. Books are written for tenure. So what? Often the sense of inquiry and self-expression is thwarted as thinking becomes a chore. Participating in the academy becomes just a job. Resentment is omnipresent. Others struggle through, face the disintegration of their fantasies, and take the reins themselves; they come to stand alone as minds. This is the calling of the Enlightenment—thinking for oneself. This is what education ideally should provide. This is what some acquire—those who carry the reins. The conflict in inquiry mirrors the concern for humanity.

We educate our population to attain the right habits of civil life. Education, like therapy, sometimes liberates; many times it does not. One would think that with all the education that academics receive they would have attained human greatness, but this is not the case. They are mostly no better or worse than people found elsewhere. Yet it seems better to think for oneself, face the problems of life, and inquire with an eye for the good and the true. This is what pedagogy tries to accomplish.

Rationality

The rational person in the present age expects and accepts this human condition, a precarious world in the acquisition of knowledge—a real world to engage. To be in good faith in inquiry (and in life more generally) is to accept the world as contingent and our position in it as precarious. There are no absolute foundations or overarching perspectives. Foundations and authorities exist, but are not absolute and should be taken much more lightly. One is forced to think for oneself, to make difficult choices, and have the courage for action.

We live with many frameworks, some compatible and some not. Our beliefs and our routines of life are all up for change. Some are more entrenched with funded wisdom than others, but as Dewey understood it, "The Quest for Certainty" is truly to be relinquished.[7] The recognition of this fact in the community of inquirers is very important. If it begins there it may be spread to other communities. In a sense it has. "Fallibilism" is the key word, as Peirce argued, but it goes against many of our desires for certainty, safety, and thoughtlessness. The acceptance of uncertainty is asking a lot of most people.

To be rational is to participate in a number of communities—to speak a number of languages or participate in a number of "language games" (chapter 2). Reason connects the various worlds and seeks unity and coherence, but not at the expense of a dominant, dogmatic one. The tyranny of a dominant one is minimized by the pluralism encountered by the competing interests of different communities. Each has a voice, but some are more true and worthy than others. There are better reasons to accept some beliefs; the world matters. The range of discourse and understanding is extended and the conceivable fruits of inquiry are enlarged.

Pragmatic sensibility demands discourse at many different levels. The rational person is one who displays, or makes actual, this capacity. The rational person looks to understand the views of those around, and to minimize the trends of thoughtless fellows and benignly barbaric leaders. The balance sought comes out of the appreciation of the different plights—the different industries. It is only in that case that rationality can assert itself.

Leaders in Inquiry

We need statespeople or politicians to guide us by the use of their heightened inquiry and practical wisdom. They speak the languages of the people. They participate in the rites and rituals of the various communities over which they preside. The politician in inquiry is a member of each community, yet without blind allegiance to any. In the best of all possible worlds everyone should be a politician, or what Plato called a "Philosopher King." That is, we need to encourage the pursuit of political wisdom in inquiry. To the extent to which we are social, we are political by nature as Aristotle taught. The ethics of social discourse are sustained by political wisdom.

To be judicious is to have knowledge. To have knowledge is to know the meanings of the many languages spoken in inquiry. To do so in worldly form is to reach the height of human intelligence—social intelligence. Social intelligence is when one can grasp the beliefs, the intentions of others, see what their goals are, and appreciate their concerns (chapter 2). Leadership in inquiry requires this. A leader must know the facts, the conditions that organize peoples' likes, the languages they speak, the habits that are entrenched and the beliefs that guide their everyday life. With such knowledge a leader perhaps, can do the right thing and make the right kinds of decisions. This knowledge is a prerequisite for being effective. It takes work and sacrifice.

This is not an advocacy of a dominant individual or group. We guard against that, not all but most of the time. Not everyone wants to be a leader, but avenues for participation must be opened, a case for the community must be fostered, and the transcendence of egoism must be encouraged.[8] The inquirer must identify with the community without being a slave to it, and must value the enhancement of the community of inquirers. Unfortunately, most will not. Still, despite this "the essence of man is contained only in the community and unity of man with man."[9]

The leader or statesperson in the community of inquirers can do one very important thing—guard against tyranny and injustice, thus reducing the chances of anyone becoming dominant. Even making judicious judgments, however, is no absolute safeguard, because there is none. The situation will always remain existential and problematical—precarious, to paraphrase Dewey.

What is envisaged are many leaders gathered together at a sort of "Round Table." The call must go call out for leaders and a democracy must be established that allows the community of inquirers to create a forum for leaders. Ideally, this would elevate a sense of responsibility for all involved. The leaders would meet periodically to discuss the events of inquiry. Each individual would provide checks and balances on the others. Power is distributed to avoid abuse. The balance of powers and the establishment of just laws and institutions are some of our safeguards. We knew this was true for political systems writ large; now we must face the same fact on a smaller scale.

The recognition of the political component of inquiry may safeguard the pursuit of truth. We need good leaders to make wise decisions so that inquiry thrives. We need them to encourage people to value thought and inquiry. Good leaders help guard the "flock," keeping them as straight as possible. The context is always going to be precarious. That is why the leader always has to be a problem solver as well as a rational agent. This is no small job. The Italian word "maestro" seems appropriate in this regard. He is more than a teacher or professor. He is a leader who nurtures the life of the mind.

But leaders all too often do not have the right ideas. That is part of why their authority is radically contingent, subject to question and change and in some sense without reality. New perspectives are always a necessary ingredient, their appreciation a constant pedagogical calling, their safeguard and development the major function of the political leader. While individuals stand over and against the community as minds, they are embedded and dependent on its existence— otherwise there is the danger of the fall into idiocy. Good leaders help provide the order and, works to provoke the participation of those in the community.

Politicians evoke disgust. The term is debased and prejorative. But the politician ideally is the grand *statesperson*. The politician guides and provides order. He or she persuades the masses with subtle imagery and works to nudge them into assuming responsibility. Ideally, politicians guide toward the good through a combination of appearance and reality. The masses are educated to consider themselves as possible members of such a round table. The nobility of the endeavor is omnipresent. The leader works to get investigators to care about their communities.

The politician must bargain. Since negotiation is at the heart of political life; life is in a real sense a kind of juggling act on shifting sands. Politicians motivate, turn people around, and keep them from being too bestial. They negotiate with them; they are subtle dialecticians. They understand how to balance so that voices can be heard.

Politics then may be the true essential art. To be good at it, the leaders must have an extraordinary amount of social intelligence. They must speak a number of languages a skill necessary in the process of civilization. We need such leaders in our community of inquirers. Without the politician the community dissolves into isolated groups or clans of egocentric discourse unable to talk to each other. The extreme form of this is found in the modern age, where there are simply many languages with no connections among them. Thus in the modern age the statesman in the guidance of inquiry provides a rational voice. This is the ideal; the real is something else.

Conflict and Hope

Inquiry will always be embedded in conflict, in part because civilization is riddled with discontent.[10] We cannot satisfy all our desires. Cultivated sublimations are worthy to pursue. That is why James may have suggested diligent training in the engagement of nature as one form of sublimation. The same holds for engaging culture—the Greek dramas of Beauty, Truth, and Justice. Here inquiry and the human ascent into grand civility are connected. The discontent is reduced.

Pragmatists across the spectrum stated that conflict is often what motivates us. Conflict can move one to look for knowledge, to experience beauty and to learn. Without the "right" kind of conflict, we are unresponsive, asleep. The right kind of conflict is in recognizing that our beliefs all too often fall short and that many of them are incompatible with one another. It often feels that we can scale the height of knowledge, yet it is always a bit out of our grasp. The attainment of truth is the grand theme that keeps civilization and inquiry going.[11]

There is no absolute moment, however, when we converge on the truth. This is the dream that the modern person relinquishes. The question then is how to avoid the pathological. Pedagogy, faith and hope are all we can appeal to and refer to in order to makes a difference. Wise and intelligent leaders and good education will help.

Beliefs are then to be doubted, but not unreasonably so, and not under the guise of bad faith. Since there is no way to get around conflict as an ingredient in almost every aspect of human life, what matters then is being dialectical about the differences we encounter. Having a sense of play might help—what Peirce called "musement." It is important to play with the various ideas, muse about their implications and contemplate the worth of their consequences. The statesman in inquiry provides the much needed perspective and gently nudges the participation of those in the community, trying to move them beyond the egoism of their own individual concerns towards the goal of participating in the community of inquirers.

Denial will be the constant seduction, and withdrawal the dominant theme. Yet inquiry will go on and knowledge will accrue, despite the primitive desire for the unconscious to take over, to lose oneself and to banish rationality. To understand such facts we need to know the relationships between the social psychological issues and historical events. We should no longer overlook these facts when coming to understand the growth of knowledge and the community of inquirers. It is part of the process of protecting inquiry from the barbaric.

Conclusion

There is real human greatness in being an inquirer. The idea of inquiry is tied to a particular conception of knowledge and liberation. As inquirers, we stand alone (to some extent at least) and accept responsibility for our thoughts and actions and the direction of the community. Though not everyone is a leader, everyone to some extent bears responsibility for the trajectory of the community.

Nobody holds the key to how inquiry generally is to be guided. We know that scientism has negative connotations and that inquiry cannot be based solely on the model of physics. Also, inquiry should not be reified, but should be guided. Political wisdom and statesmanship are needed. We need wise leaders, if inquiry is to thrive in our scientific industrial age. Truth and its growth depends on them.

Chapter 7

The Sense of Inquiry Within America: Mind and Method

Introduction

This chapter discusses several distinguishing features of the American sense of inquiry (e.g., in the work of Peirce, James, and Dewey). The American sense of inquiry emphasizes both experimentation and a concept of oneself as part of nature. The emphasis is on experience, but not the passive sense of experience postulated by classical empiricism. Rather, the empiricism is radical, to paraphrase James; it is active, not passive. Inquiry and the presence of mind predominate; the vector is discovery. Intelligence is used in the widest of senses to cultivate inquiry, which then serves as a prelude for rationality, democracy and civility (chapter 2). The mood is optimistic and cultivation of the mind is the constant theme. Intelligence, wonder and musement are at the heart of the mind's activity in inquiry, but the spirit is where a hearty sense of the real predominates and science is placed in a healthy perspective. Science, not scientism is appreciated.

Historical Background: Method and Mind

There is a long tradition within America emphasizing a rich sense of experience and inquiry. This position is found in such diverse thinkers as Jonathan Edwards and Benjamin Franklin, in addition to Jefferson, Emerson, and Thoreau.[1] Edwards' theology, for example, was grounded in empiricism and experience. His great theological and philosophical work was preceded by work on the biology of insects. The whole American experience was one of experiment; thus it is not that surprising that the prominent thinkers would exemplify it in what they did.

Benjamin Franklin was the founder of the first intellectual society in America, "The American Philosophical Society: For Promoting Useful Knowledge." Franklin appreciated that methodological innovation is essential for epistemological advances. The roots of inquiry are perhaps found here with the emphasis on method. While Franklin himself was a chronic inventor, he also emphasized education and founded what became The University of Pennsylvania.[2]

The third president of the Philosophical Society, Thomas Jefferson, figured no less prominently in his appreciation of inquiry. He labored many hours as an observer of nature, mapping out new territory and building new schools. He built the University of Virginia, which he designed himself. A sense of effort pervades his trajectory. Flexibility of thought was his mode of engagement and improvement of humanity was the dominant goal. These themes are the common blueprint of the American tradition of inquiry.[3]

Emerson and Thoreau stand out for their appreciation of experience and nature.[4] The emphasis of both inquirers is on the aesthetics of nature, its beauty and the elevation of the individual exemplified in solitary walks in the woods. Self-reliance and a knack for getting something done is highlighted in their descriptions of how to engage the world. These are, of course, important features of the American sense of how to be. So much seems possible. The optimism is orientated toward the grace of nature and the role of mind within it: the mind that builds and constructs makes a difference, and is to be appreciated. It is active, not passive. Emily Dickinson said, "I know a mind when I meet one," and found minds in abundance within nature.

William James

William James was an early proponent of evolution and of mind being part of nature.[5] As indicated in the introduction to the book, he reportedly founded the first experimental psychology laboratory in America and was of course the great proponent of popular pragmatism. In its weak form, as James understood it, pragmatism asserts that if a belief is helpful and works, then it is true. Ideas and their validity are assessed by their practical application and the resolution of some conflict. Of course this is cheap pragmatism, and even James wavered in his acceptance of it.

What James rightly emphasized was the action sense of mind—that mind evolved in nature and that intelligence is endemic to mind and nature. Mind is to a large extent (perhaps in its origins) about problem solving, as are life, and real-life contingencies. But mind is also about enjoyment. Pragmatists emphasize problem solving in addition to the enjoyment of the mind (e.g., Dewey).

The pragmatic component and the distinctive American contribution is that problem-solving is tied to the problems of life as is the mind. What James emphasized was effort and the will in problem-solving.[6] The exercised will, however, is most productively used by channelling our energies towards moral worth; that is, those beliefs worthy of merit are tied to action and the action is for some good.

James (chapter 1) valued experience, or what he called "radical empiricism." The emphasis is on the causal aspects of our mind in action. We experience the connections of events: we cause. Causation is not chimerical and is not simply what the mind imposes—a category of thought.[7] Rather, the feeling of "causal efficacy"[8] is real for James and is part of experience. Willed action is a real event (chapter 5).

Anticipation and action predominate in the characterization of animal life for James. Selective attention, a common phrase in contemporary psychological discourse, appears quite often in James' vernacular. It is directed by the needs of pressing interests and problems. We make a difference by willing our beliefs into action (chapter 5). Will, attention, and causation are intimate and part of the active sense of mind.

James was also a good phenomenologist. He coined the phrase "stream of consciousness" to describe what takes place when our mind roams. He was always a keen observer of experience. The Principles of Psychology, referred to by Peirce as the "great work," is replete with descriptions of experience. James thought that our experiences were accessible to each other (chapter 1). Recall from chapter 1 that "The Varieties of Religious Experience" are testimony to his empirical inquiry into the experiences of others. We can know them; they are important sources of knowledge.

Importantly, and following Darwin's lead,[9] James' appreciation of experience extended to other animals (see Darwin, 1879). His acceptance of the evolutionary similarity of different species lead him to consider the experiences of other animals. He understood the evolution of the brain and its functions as exhibiting varying stages in mental function that reflect our evolutionary ascent (chapters 9 and 10). The highest mental functions are represented in the newer parts of the brain, which allow for intellectual acumen. The lower parts, or those regions that evolved earlier, are the repository of habits (chapter 9).

It thus seems apparent that James' naturalism, sense of inquiry, and characterization of the active mind are chief ingredients in the American tradition. But his mistake, as Peirce understood it, was that he made pragmatism look cheap. Pragmatism is not simply problem solving, or a theory of truth that allows one to believe anything if it works. Of course this captures something of what we mean by a hypothesis being warranted, but taken too far it can undermine important factors. Perhaps the anti-intellectual ambience of America is conducive to that type of thinking. This unnerved Peirce's strong sense of the real and changed his pragmatism into pragmaticism, so that it would not be confused with what James was saying.

Charles Saunders Peirce

Peirce, perhaps, was the first experimental psychologist in America and founded what we now call pragmatism. He appreciated the investigations of Wundt and Fechner, and his own experiments on sensation were in this tradition of physiological and experimental psychology. Peirce was interested in psychophysics. While at Johns Hopkins in the 1870s he performed experiments on visual perception. Peirce and his students at Hopkins (notably Jastrow), provided evidence for a theory of color vision in his work on "small sensation of color."[10]

In the modern age Peirce would be construed as a cognitivist. Events are interpreted with no Cartesian starting point. The given is truly a myth (chapter 3). Interpretation predominates, while all cognition is hypothetical. Fallibilism is the guiding dictum of inquiry. In modern terms, "seeing" is always interpretative (see chapters 3 and 9).

By contrast, James viewed the child's experience as one of a "blooming buzzing confusion." Another way to construe this event is that the child is not thinking yet and does not impose concepts to establish order. At first the child is largely motoric, not conceptual—moving not thinking.[11] Peirce, by contrast, viewed the child's life from the beginning as filled with thought. In other words, thought is endemic from the beginning, and modern work in developmental psychology bears this out. Children are much more competent and cognitive than Piaget and certainly James thought. Children recognize objects early. They have a variety of specialized cognitive organs for problem-solving, e.g., for recognition of faces, and of animate and inanimate objects, and for comprehension of numbers and amounts; the child, in other words, may be primitive, but does think (chapter 3).

Peirce, in fact, went to great lengths to argue against the validity of any form of intuition. Like many modern thinkers, he believed that the workings of the unconscious mind are outside our awareness and cannot be intuited (chapter 2). And against British associationism, Peirce, like James, also argued that ideas are not just copies of sensory impressions.

Cognitivism is now the dominant theme in much of psychology, and through the study of the artificial one seeks to materialize conceptions of intelligence (chapter 2). Peirce in 1887 wrote an article entitled "Logical Machines." It is a discussion of machine language and presents the rather novel idea that "every machine is a reasoning machine."[12]

There might be little or much reasoning in machines. Machines are problem-solvers that presuppose a "language of thought" in performing computations;[13] through them one inquires into the logical structure of thought.

But Peirce at times equivocated whether this logical structure of thought was pure logic divorced from psychology. He in fact devoted a lot of time in his youth studying Kant's *Critique of Pure Reason*, the great epistemological work which assumed the capacity for knowledge and discarded skepticism. Kant describes the categories, of space and time that make knowledge possible.

Peirce offered his own list of categories, which kept changing depending upon the year in which he was writing. Unlike Kant's, however, Peirce's categories at times had transcendent properties, but his pantheism allowed him to think of the world as "frozen mind." Mind is endemic to nature: the common theme of America. It is not just mental but is expressed in the way we relate to the world we live in. Peirce's view has been characterized as pragmatic-idealism. Mind is objective and the categories have real life referents in the world. There are ideal minds adapted to real worlds. In fact, mind is part of biology and is part of our problem-solving capacities that evolved.

But in the modern age we naturalize Kant and push Peirce farther. We say that without categories of thought there indeed could be no intelligible world in which to function or act. We further suggest that the categories that guide our capacity to inquire are constrained and have some evolutionary significance. Moreover, Peirce's conception of deduction, induction and abduction (or retroduction) should also be naturalized.

Deduction and induction were familar before Peirce. Deduction is a property of formal reasoning to a large extent developed by the Greeks and eventually part of the fabric of science. Induction has long been a part of the English form of inquiry. Peirce, influenced by Kant and continental rationalism, introduced a third category of the mind's operations. This was abduction or retroduction. Abduction has to do with the genesis of a hypothesis. Deduction emerges in determining the consequences of the idea, and induction in finding instances of confirmation or disconfirmation. Pragmatism requires that one find the largest sense in which an idea makes a difference; abduction is the genesis of the idea, induction its empirical test, and deduction its formal implications.

Kinds of abductive events are constrained by the way the mind is structured. Chomsky for example, suggests that the child's ideas about language are constrained by the kinds of possible abductive events.[14] These constraints are biologically based (chapter 10). We place the language of categories into a problem-solving center in which our capacity to arrive at the right hypothesis in abductive moments is not haphazard or purely inductive. That is, abduction, deduction and induction evolved in animals that solve a variety of problems.

New problem solving emerges as an activity of the mind when our belief-guiding habits prove ineffectual or break down; that is, when real doubt that is based on a problematic situation emerges, inquiry and learning begin. Cartesian doubt, by contrast, exists in a vacuum: everything is doubted to attain knowledge of anything, and security comes in the form of a distant metaphysical God. Thus real-life dilemmas are avoided. Peircian doubt is tied to resolving conflicts that we face when our beliefs and habits fail us. Then we search for new ones. The event is clearly tied to problem solving.

It is interesting to note that modern learning theory construes learning as often occurring when expected outcomes fail to materialize. It is the discrepancy from our anticipations that provokes learning (chapters 2 and 8). That is true in Peirce's notion of inquiry. Through the process of inquiry we attempt to accept the loss of one set of beliefs and replace it with another. Attention is activated to a new event and learning takes place, Moreover, as does Peirce, modern learning theorists emphasize the inferences that take place in learning causal relationships.[15]

Peirce raised the possibility of a theory of semiotics. Meaning is a common occurrence of nature. Purposeful behavior, so important for the pragmatists, is endemic throughout the natural and cultural environment. In addition, animals look for signals and interpret their meanings (chapter 2).[16] And, meanings are not strictly mental. Memory also to some extent, exists independent of the mind. Categories make purposeful behavior possible. The language of problem-solving expressed by human beings and other animals has reference to the natural world in which we evolved.

Peirce was an astute reader of Lamarck, Darwin and their ideas on evolution. Biological thinking was very much a part of his world view in which the categories that organize our experience are tied to problem-solving. His colleague, Chauncey Wright, had made Kantian conceptions of space and time part of the mental fabric in the theory of the evolution of the mind; that is, our conceptions of space, time, and causation evolved with that of problem solving.[17] Peirce's realism about matter and mind allowed him to think of them as co-evolving; therefore, his epistemology was tied to evolution. Problem-solving capacities represent specific adaptations in our evolutionary past, at least in some contexts (chapters 2 and 10).

But Peirce was not a Darwinian; he remained a steady Lamarckian. Biological change had something to do with the experience of wanting, and this had consequences for biological adaptation. Perhaps Peirce's reluctance to accept natural selection was because he envisioned evolution as a step upward toward a higher state of civilization. After all, he did believe in what he called "evolutionary love"—a community coming together to share their love of kindred spirit. In fact, Peirce always emphasized the role of community, particularly in what he called the "growth of reasonableness." This is essential to the development of civilization and begins in biology.

Peirce had an appreciation for rigorous methodology and for scientific psychology, but was not scientistic. Science was not the prime value. For Peirce (and James), the world of knowledge was larger than science. Peirce thought that a community of inquirers would eventually agree upon truth over the long haul. He believed that the self-correction method of science was an important factor and was one of the first scientist-philosophers to appreciate fully how science works. True hypotheses as well as our theory-based actions are related to the nature of the world and our minds. Co-operation among inquirers, the convergence of methods that tests our ideas rigorously, and the regulative nature of inquiry would insure the emergence of truth, defined for Peirce as what the future community finally decides is the case.

John Dewey

Dewey perhaps presents the clearest expression of the American sense of inquiry and experience. His work is biologically based and rooted in psychology.[18] For Dewey, our minds are tied deeply to nature and our precarious inter-actions with it. Intelligence allows us to cope, take charge and to have pleasure in things not beyond our control. But problem solving, an active part of our being (chapter 2), is not everything.

Dewey emphasized the search for stability which is at the heart of his theory of intelligence, aesthetics, and the logic of inquiry.[19] As it was for Peirce, inquiry for Dewey begins when routines, habits, or modes of problem-solving break down. This is the search from the indeterminate to the determinate: from the problematic to the resolved. Learning now takes place to a greater extent than usual.

While what motivates inquiry is discomfort that seeks a solution, there is also a consummatory aspect motivated by some need. This a common occurrence in nature. For example, animals search for food when they are hungry; the consummation is the ingestion of food. The aesthetic aspects of experience, appetitive and consummatory phases, are paramount for Dewey, and have their origin in inquiry and problem-solving. When an answer is obtained from a set of problems, the experience is pleasurable or consummatory. This is what Dewey meant by a consummatory experience (see chapter 8). But pragmatists like Dewey, so action-orientated, gave little importance to meditative experiences.

Dewey also understood logic not as a formal discipline but tied to our daily lives.[20] His sense of empiricism was large, not narrow and positivistic, and his large notion of inquiry was tied to his sense of truly valuable "funded wisdom," the essence of the mind's life. Inquiry itself is one of our prized senses. Without it we wither into dead habit and dogmatic allegiance. With it the universe offers innumerable possibilities. What is ultimately important is not a fact, but the process of inquiry by which we search for knowledge.

Finally, Dewey, like his fellow pragmatist Mead,[21] emphasized the social factors that dominate life. His emphasis was on education and clearing out the sterility of the museum approach to the growth of the mind. The knowledge of beauty, like truth and morality, is an active process that begins in the classroom of the larger world; thus, the growth of intelligence, through the active engagement of one's surrounding, is what insures democracy and civility (chapters 2 and 6). Dewey perhaps naively overvalued problem-solving, the cultivation of which he saw as necessary for democracy and all that we value as part of our inherited funded wisdom.

Pragmatism: Inquiry and the Modern Age

The sense of inquiry in America is related to the sense of adventure into a new world and exploration into new terrain. In America, practical solutions were needed to adapt to new surroundings. The pioneers were forced to rely on themselves to create simple, workable ideas. This was and still is a future-orientated, pragmatic culture in which rolling up one's sleeves and confronting problems in a concrete fashion matters more than ideology.

Of course the down side is that America maintains an anti-intellectual climate. Europeans and others have nearly always seen Americans as anti-intellectual, and there is no doubt some truth in this assessment.[22] But for all the Europeans' sophistication, they perhaps lose access to the innocence one needs for sustained inquiry. After all, the fall into cynicism occurs when the sophisticated see the futility of action. It is the naive person who often takes the risk. Cultivated naiveté grounded in funded wisdom should be the guiding principle. It is enough, however, to be connected to a culture that appreciates ideas. European, Asian, Hispanic and African cultures, breathes new intellectual life, into American culture on a regular basis.

Method does seem to dominate in America (in education, in science, in law), at times at the expense of ideas. This lends itself to scientism—that science is all of knowledge and that all forms of inquiry follow one protocol (chapter 1). When method dominates, it lends itself to idiocy by exaggerating the scope of the method and undervaluing ideas that led to the development of the method. That is, such an overevaluation of method undercuts thought. But it is thought that generates methods.

Ideally, inquirers are not scientistic. While they appreciate science, the notion of inquiry is larger than that of science. What they have is a real sense of the world. The scope of inquiry is vast and open-ended and represents an attitude about life that requires a certain amount of humility, and that perhaps has its roots in a religious sense of wonder about the world and its mysteries. We should appreciate what growth there is in knowledge, and there is growth (chapter 6).

While emphasis has been placed on naturalism it is not a monolithic perspective. An inquirer justifiably asserts that we see ourselves as emerging from nature and influenced by our evolutionary past. Pragmatists were very responsive to this fact.[23] This is also reflected in the categories that the mind imposes to produce order.

Many inquirers have made this point that cultural categories are large determining factors for how we experience and understand the world—our world—the shared human world. There is no issue about this. They also provide order for our shared outlook and experiences, and are reflected by the world that we live in, interact with and adapt to. But the world (nature-culture) is the measure for our warranted assertions.[24] We also look to nature and how we adapt to our surroundings for the categories we impose. We need a concept of the real (chapters 3 and 10) from the external world, and not just from within ourselves.

For a pragmatist, the world is filled with purpose and meaning.[25] There is no fixed universe. A sense of process predominates, and the world is engaged. While reason does merge with culture (chapter 2) the mental frame that makes this possible evolved with intelligence. While most things that are specially human are related to language, and tied to culture, this does not mean that everything we posit is a social construction.

It was fashionable several years back to argue that gender, for example, is a social construction. This was at a time of great change when the gender relationships were being challenged. Women and men could transcend their roles. The roots for this may be found perhaps in the work of Margaret Mead, who through her travels developed and supported a pluralistic world view.[26] But, in the middle 1970s she herself said that the gender issue had gone too far; women were indeed the ones who reproduced and who often built the nests. Genetic mechanisms are responsible for the sexual characteristics of animals. Indeed, there is great plasticity in how we express our gender-related differences, but the differences are surely there. Their existence is not just a cultural artifact, though, to be sure, the culture we live in influences its expression. This is what Mead was suggesting.

Moreover, our capacity to cooperate with one another reflects our biology. We are social animals by nature and necessity; that is, we are social and political, as Aristotle long ago noted. Evolutionary factors selected for social cooperation. Culture and the development of reason then figured in its various forms of expression.

The humanities, therefore, include the sciences; they are part of the expression of human creativity.[27] For someone like James, the idea of being educated was that one became a good person, and could see it in others. A cultured person was a dignified person, not a snob with pretensions. Rather a civilized human being is a big person of heart, where what is expressed are the finer graces of human expression at the foremost of one's actions. Culture makes this possible.

Indeed, culture is no less basic than biology—the two interwine at every step. James, for one, was keenly aware of this, and to harness the basic biological instincts towards good actions. C. Judson Herrick the great comparative neuro-anatomist, suggested ". . .the human cerebral cortex is the specific organ of civilization. . . ."[28] It was through evolution that brain and mind developed (chapters 9 and 10).

Cultural and biological categories often have no perfect fit or representation with the world. This fact for the inquirer is empirical, not ideological. Moreover, the fact that natural categories may come first in terms of phylogeny does not mean that they are more important than categories that derive from culture.

In addition, when one thinks about the evolution of the mind one considers not only the phylogenetic past, but also the development of past civilizations. Thus while we evolved in nature, we also evolved in culture. So did our expression of inquiry. While its roots are in problem-solving for survival, innate curiosity obviously contributed to its creation.

Conclusion

The American sense of inquiry is unique. From the beginning it was tied to invention and methodology; methodo-logical innovations invoke epistemological advances. But methodology is blind without good ideas; in fact, there is no methodology without thought. From Franklin through Peirce, simple techniques were tested and healthy empiricism was expressed.[29]

The American energy and its rebellion against authority were important components in the development of inquiry. Individualism coupled with a sense of wonder are cardinal features with engineering as the dominant theme. But the concept of engineering is wide in scope and encompasses the widest use of intelligence (Dewey). At its best, inquiry is based on ethics and aesthetics, self control and conduct.[30] Values are not something in the head, but out there in the world. To be at all is to have some value (chapter 2). The American tradition of inquiry emphasizes the pleasures of discovery and the will to push civilization by the results. Inquiry, along with social intelligence allows us to participate in the community and to transcend the isolation of solitary thought.

Chapter 8

The Emergence of Aesthetic Experience

Introduction

This chapter is about aesthetic fulfillment, learning, and aesthetic inquiry. Aesthetics and its appreciation in the psychobiology of everyday life was noted by Peirce, James and Dewey. My thesis is that a basic form of aesthetic experience evolved from movement dancing. As one author put it "All dance is originally...of intense excitement and increased activity;"[1] another said "...the first true art is dance."[2] Within this aesthetic experience we encounter the entire drama of experience, hypothesis testing and pragmatism. In other words, inquiry and action.

The first step in its defense is to analyze Kant's concept of the sublime, which generated important ideas for understanding aesthetic experience, and to naturalize it as a pragmatist would do. The next step is to argue that movement is one of the origins of the enjoyment of the sublime. The final step is to show how the general thesis is illustrated in the phenomenon of choice, song and development. The final section relates the thesis to culture and health.

Kant and Aesthetics

Kant thought of the sublime as a particular experience of nature requiring aesthetic concepts. But the aesthetic concepts cannot quite capture the infinity of great mountains, valleys, or trees. According to Kant, the sublime is "...the

107

representation of which determines the mind to think the
unattainability of nature regarded as a presentation of ideas."[3]
The fact that we cannot wholly represent nature instills in
us an appreciation of nature's sublime infinite magnificence,
revealed in the application of concepts that do not quite
capture nature.

Aesthetic judgments themselves are made within what
Kant called the "free play" of the imagination. It is through
the appreciation of beauty that one begins to "see" a teleology
in nature. But there is no over-arching sense to be made of
nature's magnificence. We cannot quite capture it; nature's
magnificence eludes our limited understanding. All attempts
at painting, writing, composing, fall short. There is something
existential about this predicament. The failure of representation evokes an experience of the sublime. As Kant understood it ". . .the feeling of the sublime brings with it as its
characteristic feature a movement of the mind. . . ."[4] The
experience reveals something of our minds to us.

For Kant, the sublime is not the same as the beautiful.
The former is tied to nature, and the latter is tied to culture.
The distinction is itself troublesome. But contrast the magnificence of the ocean, dolphins jostling amidst a setting sun
and a full moon in the background, with a Japanese garden
carefully sculptured with perfect regularity. In the latter case,
our concepts capture its form; one can understand it. In the
former case we witness the expanse and stand awed. Yet we
persist in trying to reach a level and perfection of understanding that exists beyond what is cognitively possible. So
while beauty is perhaps about attainable perfection within
our grasp, the sublime is about unattainable striving for
magnificence.

Form and Struggle

The animal's body is designed to achieve some purpose,
reach some shape, and achieve biological functions. A
panorama of sensory input motivate the movements. The
animal subconciously strives to move well. Aesthetic judgments that are tied to intention and function guide and

organize the animal's movement. It sets out to achieve a form of expression by applying concepts (or in this case representations of bodily movements) for which there are no perfectly suited movements. The discrepancy is noted. This experience motivates the desire for finer movement in achieving better form. A struggle persists; on occasion, good form is achieved. A sense of the sublime then emerges. At times, the struggle is minimal, and the enjoyment is maximal.

Conflict is often, but not always necessary. There is, of course, the desire and enjoyment of just mastering the body. In development, the child enjoys the mastery of his or her body.[5] The sublime begins to appear in an early context, but its existence is ephemeral and short-lived, like a dance. Nonetheless, the animal strives to express itself through its body, and therein emerges the experience of the sublime. It is basic and biologically salient.

Movement and Dance

It is known that the chimpanzee will "dance" in certain rhythms. Kohler describes the movements of the chimpanzee as suggesting "primitive stages of dancing," and "the resemblance to a human dance became truly striking when the rotations were rapid, or when Tschego, for instance stretched out horizontally as she spun around."[6]

As Armstrong has stated, "dancing of one kind or another is characteristic of so many creatures from spiders to apes. . ."[7] The author also notes that bird dances and human dances have some of the same characteristics. The phenomenon of humans imitating birds and other animals is well-known.

At first the animal dance is triggered by ecologically relevant stimuli. The brain is prepared to receive certain messages, e.g., specific movements, sounds, or sights. These stimuli initially trigger movement. But eventually the animal wants to move, decides to move and a sense of play emerges. The same holds for the child in development. The child wants to express his or her body and use his or her muscles.

Evolution has produced active mental organs to assume control over human and animal bodily expressions. The categories that organize behavior are part of the natural biology of the animal. The body is then given shape through its exercise through *bodily inquiry*. The movements have the shape they have because of the mentality to which they conform and the environments to which they are adapted. The movements become ritualized creatively into dance forms.

The struggle for better form provokes more enjoyment as the dancer gets closer to achieving the form. It also leads to disappointment and despair which is internal to the dancer. There are also aesthetic judgments that are external, the attraction to and enjoyment of the dancer's movements by an audience.

Viewing Others

There is experimental evidence that a chimpanzee prefers to view the movements of a good dancer over a bad one, a fine walker over an awkward walker, that it would rather watch a film clip of a beautiful movement over one less beautiful.[8] These results suggest that the animal makes aesthetic judgments of others. The animal's understanding of movements, whatever they are, makes this possible.

Nature selects for fitness and for what works—the pragmatic. But we feel pleasure rummaging through the trees, or in dancing, or whirling on the top and into the water (a whale) or in flying in certain motions (a bird). We take pleasure in our own expression. We watch the movement of others express their fitness. Good movement is vital for survival, which is why it is fundamental and why the experience of the sublime is tied to it.

Communicative Movements

The dance is also often a communicative act, e.g. as in the dance of one bee signaling that food is to be found in a location to other bees.[9] The dance attracts and is binding to other bees.

Communicative dance is particularly striking in the courting displays of animals. Watch the male pigeon in the streets and parks of New York City perform his ritualized courtship dance. His neck bulges. His head bobs and weaves. He circles beautifully. He attracts, or tries to. The female pecks at food while the male keeps dancing, pumping himself up more and more. From a finite set of ritualized actions, biologically given, the bird attempts to attract the female.

The more creatively the male combines the movements, the greater the possibility of attracting the female. The individual bird demonstrates his own flair, or fails to. The result is copulation, or frustration. It is amazing that they ever reproduce; he is always dancing, while she is always eating. But it happens and new birds are hatched. The act itself is a rewarding process—it feels good to the pigeon.

In such contexts, one notices direct relationships between the expression of the body, the sexual attraction, and the reproductive potential. In enticing a spouse and reproducing, the animal's fitness is determined. Fitness of form predominates in the selection. A concept of the sublime is present in the very natural domain of trying to perfect action through the body.

The relationship of actual movement to its ideal representation is a sensed imperfect fit. There is a desire for a better fit, and the resulting action may eventuate in creative movement; that is, the animal creatively uses its resources to attain the ideal more nearly. The result can be a novel form of bodily expression in both the reception (the judgment of others) and presentation of movement. The novel form emerges through what Kant calls the "free play of the imagination", or in the present context through the imaginative use of bodily representations. This mental act expresses itself in the orchestration of new movements from possible forms resulting in a novel movement. The extent to which an animal expresses itself is related to the creative implementation of representations of bodily forms. The extent to which the animal achieves the ideal bodily form corresponds to the experience of the sublime and its enjoyment. The animal is motivated to achieve and fulfill action through bodily forms of excellence.

Pleasure

Hedonic components are present in animal life.[10] Approach and avoidance responses are built into our biology.[11] The creative use of representations of bodily forms is also built into animal life, and as such so is the resultant enjoyment in fitness. The fitness of the body's movements to representations helps to insure survivability.

Expectations and their satisfaction help to organize the behavior. On a pragmatist's account, when an expectation of a represented form is not realized, inquiry, learning or enjoyment may result.[12] Habits of action are readily formed. When habitual movements become dead rituals, choice and creativity tend to be lost. But when an expectation is not realized, the viscera are aroused, and alternative patterns are entertained by the animal. The animal comes to life and generates alternatives, which require the process of thinking in action. The breakdown of the expectation of reaching some form arouses a search. There are choice, action, and inquiry directed toward the resolution of the conflict. A new means is sought to satisfy the arousal. A consummatory experience is desired. The disruption provokes a compensatory response to equilibrate. When the equilibration is achieved, pleasure is experienced. Satiation and relief are the results. The breakdown has generated an awareness, and subsequent breakthrough that trigger some sense of the sublime in both the reception and presentation of movement. Satisfaction emerges when the bodily experience fits the imagined form.

Conflict is at the heart of the search, though not necessary for it. But conflict often generates action; both enjoyment and learning often occur after the conflict of an expectation breaking down. The application of concepts that fit imperfectly helps to organize new action, that is, the lack of fit generates motivation and action.

Choice and Action

Perhaps, one comes into the world with representations of possible body movements. These representations provide the organization for movement. The creative moment is, essentially, a choice from this set of possible movements.

Habits of movement are entrenched through experience. Animal bodies are prepared to move in certain ways. As indicated, initially specific stimuli may trigger the movements, which may be elaborated upon by maturational sequences within the animal. The animal then may begin to select from the available bodily movements. If emerging habits of movement are useful, this probably gains emphasis in the animal's repertoire of possible movements. But if such movements become solidly entrenched, such that choice disappears, so may the animal. When the routine is diversified, the animal again adjusts creatively because it has to choose again. Striving also re-emerges, as does the possibility of greater fitness. Once again, there may be creativity and enjoyment. The motivation generates action, which is an attempt to resolve a dilemma and find fitness of form. The resolution is consummatory and is avidly pursued because the experience can be enjoyable and can lead to the sublime.

The sublime emerges and elevates. It appears with the body leaping in the air or flying through the trees in trying to reach bodily form. A basic form of enjoyment emerges from movement and physical expression.

Song and Movement

The sense of the sublime, or aesthetic inquiry, may be apparent in movement but it is also discernible in song. Birds, for example, appear to derive pleasure from the songs they sing.[13] The pleasure, in part, is what motivates them to sing. The bird calls out to others. The song attracts. The event is semiotic because messages are expressed and understood. Innate representations of song are creatively manipulated, resulting in a unique song, a particular physical expression. The song itself is made possible because innate song forms are creatively manipulated by the bird.

Birds manipulate abstract templates; the rules of birdsong that organize the production and the reception of the song;

specialized brain mechanisms organize the song production and reception.[14] As the bird matures the body generates endogenous rhythms that make it responsive to the song of its conspecifics. In doing so, it manipulates the abstract possibilities and instantiates them imperfectly. The inference is that the bird recognizes this (though not consciously) and is motivated to sing better. This consummatory event is pleasurable. While aesthetics may have origins in movement, it becomes part of song and becomes disassociated, or separated, from movement, culminating in language and culture.

As indicated, in animals, pleasure-seeking is a basic motivation. Therefore, in calling out to the other and hearing responses from the other, there is enjoyment, or no enjoyment. The approach—avoidance behavioral mechanisms are tied to changes in hedonic judgments and in brain mechanisms that organize these motivational events. Nature ties such processes to the business of survival. In the case of song, the song is sung loudly and beautifully because the best song attracts. The bird is "moved" to sing. The sound's production and reception in turn generates movement. The song of music serves the dance initially. It can be heard and attract from a distance. The attractiveness of the song generates the movement to approach. As one approaches, the bodily form gets expressed because of the mix of uncertainty and anticipation.

Interlude

To summarize, aesthetic inquiry may have some of its origins in movement. The body is full of endogenous rhythms that help organize the movements of the limbs, pharynx, etc. These oscillations help make movement and song possible. They can be entrained or influenced by natural contingencies, though they have their own endogenous rhythms. One motivation to move with skill and beauty is the interest in conforming movements to their representations. This is coupled with the pleasure of using a resource creatively. The interest is possible because the animal has abstract forms that guide and become instantiated in movement (or song). The poor fit of the form in a real life bodily context generates conflict or discrepancy. A shortcoming occurs. If the discrepancy is to be overcome, the animal must search and find new ways to express itself. It must *inquire*. In the process, enjoyment is or is not achieved. The enjoyment that may result motivates further physical expression. There is development, as physical prowess emerges. The bodily expression reaches for fulfillment and the emergence of the aesthetic fulfillment.

Ontogeny and Therapy

Mind develops through the creative use of form in matter. The child recapitulates the evolution of mind in body and enjoyment by first developing the use of the body for knowledge, exploration, and pleasure. The child initially inquires and learns about the world through movements that are triggered by environmental stimuli and endogenous motor programs. In later development conceptual events become separated from bodily expression, analogous to song becoming disassociated from its function in movements.

The child's early world is no "blooming buzzing confusion." The infant's world is ordered by concepts such as space, time, and faces—by representations in the mind (recall chapter 3). As I indicated psychologists have long noted that the early stages of development are characterized by operations that are bodily in nature. Pragmatists like James, but also Peirce and Dewey, have emphasized the experience of the body and the acquisition of knowledge. But other philosophers have also suggested that a primary mode of knowledge is by bodily exploration.[15] It is only later in development that mind is disconnected from the body.

Teaching people to learn about themselves through the exploration of their bodies may serve the process of inquiry.[16] Movement is easily noticed and is concrete in experience. It is also more accessible to understanding than words are. Words are more abstract than movements. In coming to understand ourselves it may be useful therapeutically to go from the more primary (the bodily) to the more abstract. There is an analogous phenomenon in the therapy for people with reading difficulties. In recapitulating the evolution of reading the therapy goes from literal bodily representations of objects to more abstract, phonetic ones.[17] The more easily accessible are the more bodily representations; having captured these one can then move on to the more abstract ones. The first step is the basic one—the body.

Biological events are not usually pathological. Habits can become pathological. But habitual movements set in and break down. Their breakdown is a mixed blessing generating discomfort, but also leading to a new feeling of satisfaction. Let us turn now to cultural bodies.

Mind and Body

Human beings are often detached from their bodies through cultural factors. In some cultures it is not so pronounced; in others it is pathological. Their bodies are like alien objects—someone else's body. This is not a natural animal condition. Animals are built to embody themselves. But humans can and do detach from their bodies, and when they do, they lose touch in part with reality. This loss can eliminate choice. Sometimes the loss of touch is good when it moves one beyond the real. But embodiment is a natural goal of life, not detached mind or disembodied bodies, but minds and bodies in unison. The unison is a result of the process of the progression of mind in body. More possibilities emerge. Ironically, with more freedom there comes the possibility of detachment from the body.

Recall the traditional dualism of mind and body discussed in chapter 3. Mind is radically free and the freedom is terrifying. The body, by contrast, is dumb, determined and unconscious. Mind looks out on the world and can choose to be whatever it wants. While bodies are in the world and determined by facts, minds are transcendental. Minds constitute; bodies do not.

The traditional dualism lends itself to a philosophic rejection of the body. Natural acts tend to be debased. Sartre describes the act of ingesting food as one of destruction.[18] He describes a woman's vaginal opening as a hole to be filled—the desire to be complete. The body, on this view, turns out to be foul, seductive and ruining.

It is easy to see how the body is often seen as depraved in our culture. It is debased in a traditional Western view. Action or desire expresses privation of being. When one is full, there is no need to move. Since desire emerges from the body, desire is to be avoided. It ruins people. To be complete, entails a mind radically disassociated from the body. Moreover, the body in our culture is often construed as passive and the mind as active, creating the mind-body problem in which the body has no essential being. The mind was cultivated; the body was discarded. But we have come to see this as bad metaphysics and a mistaken epistemology.

It is suggested that the body is active as the mind embodies it (see also chapters 9 and 10). The body is no longer solely inert, or a tropism. Choice is operative and therefore, existential. It is also tied to action. Hedonic motivational mechanisms help organize the body. If an event is painful, we stop and move to avoid it. If it is pleasurable, we stay or approach it. Approach and avoidance mechanisms are tied to the hedonic judgments we make. To take possession of ourselves is to feel the mastery of having mind in body, and in harmony. This means ascending away from a fear of movement to an appreciation and development of what Whitehead called our "causal efficacy," and to exercise the capacity to choose, move, and take pleasure. To be in one's body is not to fall into sin or depravity. The body is not evil. The mind does not need to be purified, but to be connected to the body.

In the modern period, dualism predominated the understanding of the mental. The mental was one kind of substance and the physical quite another. This position gave way in the twentieth century to identity theories in which conceptions of the mental were about the physical—the brain. The mind *is* the brain in this view.[19] Both views are extreme. Substance dualism leaves one in epistemological embarrassments.

Identity theories on the other hand, are flagrantly chauvinistic—they often deny the reality of the mental.

Mind is not the same as body. Mental functions may be embodied in a variety of different kinds of physical substances —cells or silicon. Pain is not the same as the firing of a neuron, though dependent upon physical embodiments. In the functionalistic view, one tries to determine relationships between mental functions and bodily events, or between bodily events and mental events. There is no simple bifurcation of the mental from the physical or the shameful elimination of the mental from the physical. Mind in body is basic to animal life (see also chapters 9 and 10).

The metaphysics places mind in nature, in animal life, and in bodies. As a result, the existential real-life choices, and the pleasures and pangs that go with them, are tied to pragmatic movement and action. The mind is in the body.

When we lose contact with the body, we lose our basic perceptual frame. The body receives the world(s) we inhabit and is our basic means for determining the external world. Initially, we move in order to inquire and know, and we think in order to move better. The more graceful we are, the better the movements. The better the movement the better we feel. The better we feel, the better we are likely to survive. The greater the attunement, the larger the understanding.

In fact, creative bodily use is a progenitor of other sources of creative expression and enjoyment. While the cultivation and nurturing of the body is a basic biological fact, cultivating the mind is a basic cultural fact. But in point of fact, the mind is pervasive in biological events. Though the mind may become something separate it is tied deeply to the body for its health. The separateness of the mind and the body allows us to explore a mental space independent of physical instantiations. We do not always have to move. But on the other hand, remaining stationary can lead to a detachment from the very heart of our existence—our bodies. The body and its development are tied deeply to a concept of health: the body providing the origins of enjoyment and the sublime. To lose that is to lose ourselves, to lose a deep sense of enjoyment, to lose nature.

Culture and Health

Think of Zen masters walking through forests, not disturbing the terrain yet engaged with nature. They seem very tied to their bodies. One gets this sense in the Chinese dance defensive movements of Tai-Chi-Chuan.[20] The goal is to embody the mind in the body, resulting in quiet power. There is no ontological split between mind and body. The goal is the mind's harmony with the body. A natural prowess emerges with a strong quiet sense. The picture is romantic, but it does capture something about mind in body and its prowess.

In our culture it is in the extreme when the body is called upon, that a concern for the body emerges. One takes hold of one's body, the body's importance having become manifest. Old bodily habits are broken down. One begins to be connected to the basics, to reassemble oneself, take hold and gather oneself—and return to the body.

When animals are beseiged, they tend to cleanse themselves. A dog sick with cancer develops welts on its belly. The dog licked the welts, cleansing itself, or at least trying to. Surely there is something biologically basic about this. Culture often removes us from it, and disconnects mind from body.

Finally, Moses Maimonides, a doctor and philosopher of the twelfth century, stressed the importance of keeping both the mind and the body healthy.[21] He cultivated Greek harmony of mind and body, unlike the Roman glorification of mindless bodies. While the mind is not the same as the body, Maimonides realized that mind and body both require sustenance. The mind constitutes a body, embodies it, and brings it to life. We are minds in bodies, naturally endowed with certain prowesses. The body is the medium by which we move through and inquire about the world, and as the mind is part of the body to varying degrees of fitness, so do we attain varying levels of enjoyment or the experience of aesthetic fulfillment.

Chapter 9

Evolution, Brain, and Mind

Introduction

This chapter is concerned with neurobiological expression; specifically, how the brain and the mind set conditions for inquiry and intelligence; That is, adaptive intelligent responses are represented in the brain. They are selected for by nature and represent local adaptations; they are preconditions for inquiry. These responses are both localized and distributed at various levels of the neural axis. In fact, levels of neural function reflect stages in evolution and ontogeny. Brainstem mechanisms, in particular, in the phylogenetically older regions of the brain are designed to resolve local or specific problems.

Corticalization of function emerged during evolution and arises during development. Evolutionary considerations are therefore fundamental in understanding neural architecture and function. Our best hypothesis is that the brain is under centrifugal control (theory laden, chapter 3) and is largely a hierarchical system for the control of intelligent action.

An epistemology consistent with Peirce, James and Dewey, that is based on evolutionary factors suggests that specific problem solving is selected for by nature; that is problem solving capacities and hypothesis formation are tied to our evolutionary background. Greater use of problem solving capacities further evolved with increased neural access of the forebrain to the brainstem. That is, neural connectivity which links the forebrain with the phylogenetically more ancient brainstem constitutes part of what makes the rise of intelligence possible. The neocortex, which directs behavior, is evolution's crowning neural achievement. Despite our understanding of how brains produce intelligence and the capacity for inquiry, recent work suggests intelligence is also manifested in matter other than neural tissue, and that the "frame problem" lingers. That is, it is hard enough to get machines to act intelligently, let alone wisely.

Evolution and the Vertebrate Brain

The intelligent behavioral adaptations witnessed in nature are organized by the brain. Some behaviors are well adapted to specific niches (as discussed in chapters 2 and 10); their associated brain mechanisms are also highly specialized and they are designed to solve specific problems. That does not mean that all brain mechanisms are adaptations to specific demands. Similarly, not all animal traits are naturally selected for as adaptations.[1]

Neural specialization has been linked to the "modularity thesis,"[2] and is reminiscent of nineteenth century phrenology. Gall, Broca and Flourens assigned specialized intellectual or adaptive capacities to specific brain regions. Each region of the cortex was linked to a behavioral function.[3] The localization of function thesis, however, was not widely accepted.

There is clearly localization of function in the brainstem. Simpler animals are relatively fixed in what they can do. The primitive base of the brains of animals like ourselves is the brainstem, and basic sensory, cardiovascular and visceral functions are localized there.[4] Each piece solves a specific problem.

However, as one moves up from the brainstem to the more recently evolved forebrain, one finds less localization of function. At least this is how it must have appeared to the early investigators, whose discoveries led them to reject localization of intellectual functions, and to theorize that the whole of the cortex is involved in intelligent functions.[5] But we now know that sensory and other functions, e.g., language, are localized in the cortex.[6]

Hughlings Jackson, a noted British neurologist influenced by Herbert Spencer's evolutionary theories, envisioned the brain in terms of levels of function rather than simple localization of function.[7] He saw the elaboration of brain tissue as a physical correlate of evolution. Each level represented a stage in the evolution of the brain, behavior, intelligence and the capacity to solve problems—to inquire.

An important point in this regard is the notion of dissolution (as briefly mentioned in chapter 5). Damage to the cortex or other recently evolved tissue renders one more reflexive, and less able to adapt to novel situations. Thus Jackson noted that his patients with cortical damage were able to perform simple motor responses such as sticking out their tongues to gustatory stimuli, but could not do so on command. He took this as evidence that the control of such reflexes proceeds from the cortex (or other more evolved neural tissue) down to the brainstem.

The study of memory has corroborated the Jacksonian message that the earlier the information enters memory, the more likely it will be retained and made more prominent following brain damage, dementia or senility.[8] That is, the first behavioral functions learned are the ones that remain as the brain deteriorates. For example, polygots frequently revert to the language of youth, despite the fact that the majority of life was spent not speaking that language, and possibly not even recalling it during this time.

Jackson's mistake was his assumption that "the whole nervous system is a sensori-motor mechanism."[9] He failed to realize that one could hold materialistic premises and still have a concept of the mind as something more than a sensory-motor integrator. We now believe that the brain thinks, and that something as seemingly simple as sensory motor integration requires thought, or a background theory (chapter 3). Jackson's other point is well accepted. Moving up the brain, one can find differential control over a system at higher levels of organization that is re-representing the lower levels (e.g., gustatory representations).

The emotional responsiveness of animals with different amounts of neural tissue left intact following neural transection was studied. Animals without the cortex displayed what Bard and others called "sham rage."[10] Sham rage has the behavioral components of rage without the emotion that goes with it. He also found that thalamic animals did not show goal orientated behavior. The cortex was important in being directed intelligently and was not blindly triggered. These different neural transections are sketched in Figure 1.

Bard suggested that forebrain control has not resulted in a ". . . shift of the essential management of every kind of emotional expression out of the brainstem. . . ."[11] Rather, the basic units are still in the brainstem, and the evolved tissue in the forebrain manipulates them in ever-expanding contexts of use. Similarly, the basic units for ingestive behavior lie in the brainstem,[12] but their non-reflexive use in ever widening ingestive contexts lies in forebrain control of these brainstem units. As Bard notes, "when through the operation of evolutionary processes nature added to the brain a cerebral cortex she probably discharged very few of her old employees."[13]

Following Jackson's idea of the evolution of the nervous system, the assertions are first, that as one moves up in the brain, the brain goes from the most to the least organized at birth. Second, this corresponds to a progression from simple and relatively reflexive acts to more complex acts. Third, these complex acts appear to be those over which we have some voluntary control. Evolution adds to the existing brain mechanisms, which are designed to adapt to specific problems and contingencies that the animal may face. Damage to the forebrain reduces one to earlier stages of evolutionary capacity, with fewer options. In Jackson's vernacular, the dissolution of the brain is the reverse of evolution.

We now know that late evolution of neural tissue does not necessarily mean that it is less organized.[14] For example, new tissue that organizes motor control tends to be highly organized (motor cortex), while older tissue (striatum) tends to be less specialized.

Concepts of development are also tied to the evolution of the brain. In this view the child is something akin to a decerebrate,[15] which is a vertebrate with a disconnected

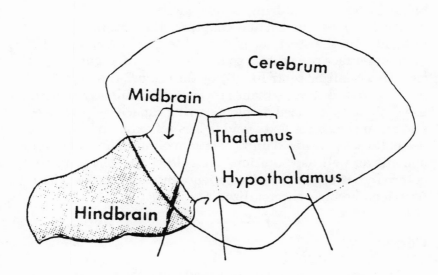

Figure 1. The brain of the cat showing various neural transections (heavy lines) (from Gallistel, 1980).

forebrain (Figure 2). As the child develops and begins to inquire, it moves up the evolutionary scale, the march of corticalization of function. In fact, the basic reflexive responses are intact in the newborn. The anencephalic child is remarkedly similar to the intact newborn although it is without a forebrain.[16] However, the normal child moves beyond the reflexive control of the brainstem as it matures. As a result, the child's behavior as it begins to inquire, is purposeful, voluntary, and under more cortical control (as discussed in chapter 5).[17] Importantly, neural connections that subserve behavior are made during development.[18]

As indicated in earlier chapters, the child's world is ordered from the start, as evidenced by specialized modular systems for face recognition spatial or temporal organization; they are organized centrifugally by the brain.[19] The important point is that as development proceeds, the child expands its use of these specialized problem-solving capacities in greater and more varied contexts, and is less reflexive in his or her use of these specialized units of organization. Thus, in development as well as evolution, the role of the cortex in the governance of behavior and experience increases as behavioral functions become encephalized.

Cortex

The cortex, in one view, awakened when the basic reflexive units in the brainstem were insufficient to perform a task or solve a problem.[20] This view mirrors the pragmatist's view of intelligent action: thought occurs when the old habits of action break down or fail to function. New thinking and cortical functions then emerge. Old habits, such as motor programs, or what Peirce called "frozen thought" are performed by older parts of the brain. The new brain is used when the old habits embedded in brainstem tissue fail. Then the more evolved brain tissue is activated by more sophisticated inquiry.

The cortex has also been thought to subserve general functions like attentiveness. In the nineteenth century, Goltz[21]

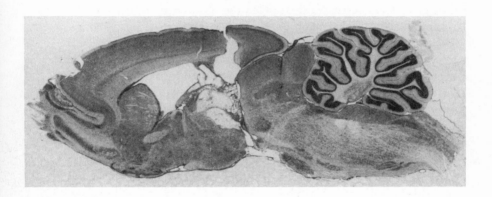

Figure 2. Representative sagittal section of the brain of a supracollicular chronic decerebrate rat (from Grill, Schulkin and Flynn, 1986).

suggested that the degree of deficit in attention to events was related to the degree of cortical damage. Karl Lashley's ideas about mass cortical action in learning are very similar.[22] In fact, learning is connected to attention.[23] As indicated in earlier chapters, the view that one learns new things by paying attention is consistent with the pragmatic view of learning and inquiry, though learning can take place without paying attention.[24]

Since the time of Jackson, the cortex has been associated with abstract thought. Abstract thought, reflecting on possible or actual events and their expected outcomes, is surely related to an advance in evolution. In fact, brain damage to the cortex renders one more concrete[25] and confined to specific adaptations.

Significantly, it was James who suggested that "all nervous centers have then in the first instance one essential function, that of intelligent action"—or problem solving.[26] But it is the cortex that renders one free from reflexive action, just as, in development, one moves away from reflexive action through corticalization of function.

This was not the view of the behaviorist, for whom the brain throughout was a reflexive organ within which new connections were made by reinforcing new associations.[27] Still it is widely believed that the cortex, by forming new sensory-motor connections, was the tissue in which learning took place. For example, associative learning and "the instinct for food and self preservation was, like all instincts located in the cerebral hemispheres."[28]

We now know that many forms of learning and instinctual responses can take place in animals that have no cortical tissue at all. Associative learning can occur in decorticates;[29] the basic units for hunger are in the brainstem, not in the cortex. Moreover, associative learning is now seen as thought or mind dependent.[30]

But how is the cortex organized? Lashley thought in terms of two concepts[31]: "equipotentiality" and "mass action." The first asserted that each part of the cortex is of equal value in subserving the same functions; that it was not specialized the way the brainstem seemed to be. The second was that the system when damaged broke down in degrees; the larger the damage to the cortex the greater the intellectual decrement. Modern models of massively parallel systems are similarly non-specialized and relatively equipotential. When the system is debilitated, the output is degraded in terms of the amount of substrate damaged.[32] This was how Lashley saw the rat cortex.

We should not, however, view the cortex and central states as isotropic, lacking the substance around which to frame a science.[33] We know that the cortex has some structure and that it is both specialized and non-specialized in carrying out intelligent action. From cytoarchitectural and functional studies we know that the cortex is under columnar organization. This means that local circuits, or modules, across the six layers of the cortex are vertically organized in the control of, for example, visual processing, with selective columns processing different aspects of visual input.[34]

This same principle holds for other cortical regions in the processing of information; that is, vertical columns in the cortex are organized into discrete units that are homogenous, responding to one modality (except for the association cortex), having both the same neural properties and the same peripheral receptive fields while being different from other units. Thus the cortex is highly specialized for information processing and has definite structure.

There is also hemispheric specialization between the two cortical hemispheres. In addition, fine grain motor control—a very specialized function ranging from tongue protrusion, to finger dexterity—emerged from neocortical tissue. There is also specialization in neocortical tissue for sensory and association areas of the cortex.[35]

Human language is also an example of a highly specialized system.[36] It is biologically based and has been associated with an anatomical locus in the neocortex for over one hundred years.

Finally, Geschwind[37] suggests that the parietal lobe of the neocortex integrates sensory information that is important in language use from many modalities. This same brain region is involved in attention. The capacity to integrate different sensory modalities is essential for language, and the parietal lobe is a region where all sensory information concerned with language converges. The parietal lobe has access to all the sensory systems. Thus there is both specific and non-specific processing of information by brain regions involved in linguistic expression.

Brain Size and Intelligence

Brain size is somewhat correlated with intelligence. The assumption is that the larger the brain the more information it can process. This has been called the "principle of proper mass."[38] However, we know that some animals with large convoluted cortices (e.g., cows) are not much brighter than some of the insects (e.g., bees) which have no cortices at all. Mass can be just bulk. But it is known that brain size increases during periods of biological importance; for example, specific nuclei in male birds increase in size during the mating season when they call out to the females to attract them.[39] Moreover, if one contrasted the intelligent performances of the octopus, rat, and dolphin they would correlate quite nicely with the size of their cortices.

Neural Connectivity and Intelligent Action

Neural connectivity helps make intelligent responses and the capacity for inquiry possible. The intermediate neural tissue between the brainstem and hypothalamus has been called the neuropil.[40] The neuropil was construed as a diffuse pathway of axons and dendrites (lumped together as a large neural web) communicating information to and from the brainstem to the more evolved brain regions. Later it was discovered that more direct neural routes such as the reticular formation or the medial forebrain bundle transmit specific and non-specific sensory and visceral information to the forebain.

Now we know that the brainstem is directly connected to the cortex, bypassing classical thalamic nuclei which were formerly seen as the intermediate stop en route to the cortex. These direct projections thereby transcend the strict hierarchy of the intermediate units in the mid-brain. In addition, the frontal cortex, or insular cortex of the neocortex, as well as the amygdala (which is old reptilian cortex), have direct projections to and from the solitary nucleus which receives visceral input from gastrointestinal and cardiovascular regions of the body. In animals like ourselves this allows for greater accessibility and control of these brainstem units. An example of such circuitry, in this case the visceral neural axis, is depicted in Figure 3.

One striking feature of the evolution of intelligence is the increasing accessibility of specialized functions for greater use in problem solving (chapters 2 and 10). A system that evolved for recognizing visual objects of certain dimensions became accessible and extended in its range of applicability. It is possible to observe this through the analysis of the neural connectivity of the brain regions and their increased neural connections during the evolutionary development of the brain. New neural connections are made, and cell assemblies are established.[41] New pathways emerge. Possibilities for *inquiry* multiply. The prefrontal cortex that projects to the motor units that control fine motor action in the brainstem, or to the visceral part of solitary nucleus which controls our cardio-vascular and autonomic reactions are examples of such pathways.[42]

Limbic System: Approach and Avoidance

Hedonic judgments are pervasive in mammalian life (chapter 8). Such judgments activate the approach toward or avoidance of objects. When we diverged from the reptilian line we developed viscerally organized motivated systems of a very different sort from our predecessors.[43] The limbic system elaborated basic motivated-emotional responses.[44] In this context the limbic system, as it evolved, assumed more control of the brain areas it was superceding, often providing an inhibitory and excitatory role in the organization of behavior, and playing an important role in the satisfaction of desires.

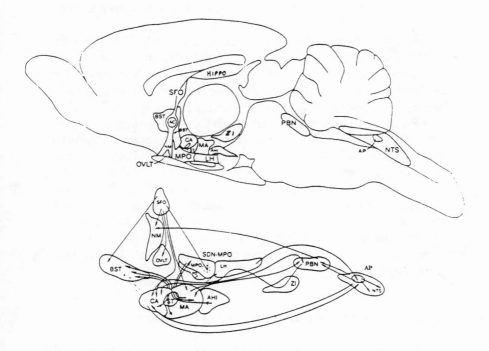

Figure 3. Depiction of the rat brain showing (above) sites of special interest of a neural circuit which controls the behavioral expression of body fluid homeostasis, and (below) major connections among them (Schulkin and Epstein, unpublished). AHI: amygdala-hippocampal regions; AC: anterior commisure; AP: area postrema; BST: bed nucleus of the stria terminalis; CA: central nucleus of the anygdala; Hippo: hippocampus; LH: lateral hypothalamus; LPO: lateral preoptic area; MA: medial nucleus of the amygdala; MPO: medial preoptic area; NM: nucleus medianus; NTS: nucleus of the tractus solitarius; OVLT: organum vasculosum of the lamina terminalis; PBN: parabrachial nucleus; SDN-MPO: sexually dimorphic nucleus of the medial preoptic area; SFO: subfornical organ; ST: stria terminalis; ZI: zona incerta.

In fact, forebrain control over reflexive responses mediated by the brainstem reveal both inhibitory and excitatory properties that are tied to approach-avoidance behaviors. We know that such inhibitory and excitatory capacities are part of the limbic system. Regions of the hypothalamus and amygdala are particularly important as central inhibitors or facilitators of behavior—that is, in approaching or avoiding objects.

Recall that the limbic system includes the prefrontal and cingulate cortex, hypothalamus, septum, hippocampus, and amygdala in addition to parts of the thalamus and the striatum.[45] The limbic system also contains specific nuclei that orchestrate different behaviors, e.g., sexual behavior and the ventral medial hypothalamus, regulation of circadian behavioral rhythms and the suprachiasmatic nucleus of the hypothalamus; and thermal regulatory behavior and the medial preoptic region. Moreover, the steroid hormones that alter the brain during development and initiate behavioral responses to homeostatic needs are localized in limbic regions.[46]

The hypothalamus (under the thalamus and part of the diencephalon) and the amygdala are important integrators in the regulation of desires and their satisfaction. Moreover, disorders of emotional-motivational expression may emanate from these brain regions. Motivation and the approach and avoidance of objects in the world occurs, in part, through limbic activation of the striatum, which organizes motor patterns, e.g., via the extrapyramidal system and its activation of well-rehearsed motor actions.[47] That is, the striatum, or extrapryamidal system, is thought to organize well-rehearsed motor patterns.

Brain Design: Centrifugal Control

Nature has selected for certain principles that organize behavior and provide order. What Peirce called abduction is our capacity to hit on the right hypothesis (chapter 7). This may occur because the range of hypotheses that we consider are constrained by evolutionary factors.

Brains are organized centrifugally and select out their own responsiveness to the world. The sensory nerves are informed by the more central structures in the brain. There is no "given" that is simply responded to by the brain. In philosophical terms, the senses are laden with theory (chapter 3). What we see, hear, etc. is under centrifugal control in neuroscientific terms. Brain mechanisms in motor control, the motor cortex, striatum, and cerebellum, are activated before the actual body movements occur.[48] The frog has command neurons in the mid-brain for catching and then eating moving objects; they inform the more peripheral units to catch and eat the moving objects. The command neurons are the centrifugal mechanisms that determine action. They impose the theory of what is out there in the world to the basic units in the brainstem and then the periphery which does the actual work.

By centrifugal order, I mean a top-down hierarchy of command in what is seen, in the interpreting of it, and in making adjustments of importance. Similarly, while the frog brain has no cortex, the same principle of centrifugal control holds. Through evolution, with the development of more brain tissue, more centrifugal control emerged.

Brain Thought: An Overview

Intelligence is endemic to the brain. Biologically oriented psychologists, like James for instance, recognized that.[49] Evolution has provided a number of brain regions for problem solving and inquiry. There is great specialization in the older parts of the brain: a massive set of modular, parallel processing systems all working on different aspects of physiological and behavioral co-ordination. But there is specialization in the newer parts as well. There is tissue in both the cortex and limbic system that is modular or nonmodular, specialized or distributed. They are both part of the great neural networks that are operative in the brain. Modular systems are not incompatible with parallel systems in the brain. How much a brain system is modular and specialized or works in conjunction with other systems is a matter of degree and is an empirical question.

As we evolved, there were a number of ways to solve problems faced in nature. Brains evolved to recognize problems, to invoke solutions, to test hypotheses using a background of knowledge, and to act quickly. Brains evolved to inquire. If the hypothesis does not work, and if the brain is sufficiently evolved, it will invoke other hypotheses to test. Problem solving is "selective trial and error."[50] The brain is thus a massive computing device.[51] It is constantly thinking, inquiring, and solving problems.

Philosophical Functionalism

An idea of the evolution of vertebrate brains has been outlined. When one turns to invertebrates, e.g. insects or slugs, the picture changes dramatically. While the vertebrate cortex may be involved in planning events to come, creatures with no cortex at all, e.g., bees, also have complicated social lives that require quite a bit of planning. Nature exploits a number of resources to attain the same function, in this case, planning. From the amoeba to little children, intelligent systems in nature adapt and generate hypotheses to resolve dilemmas, or solve local problems. All animals in some sense are like scientists; they are problem solvers.[52]

One sees here the power of philosophical functionalism. This is the idea that the material stuff out of which a function is produced can vary (chapter 1). For example, learning can take place in animals without a cortex, limbic system, or thalamus, etc. In fact, as Jennings asserted, the cortex is not necessary for learning at all. Even unicellular organisms without neural tissue can learn—and not merely reflexively. For Jennings, such primitive creatures act as if they have cortical tissue, since they are not simply stimulus-bound in their behavior and may generate and test hypotheses in adapting appropriately.

Moreover, we know that invertebrates like bees have circadian 24-hour timing devices that help to organize their temporal sense of the world, but they have no hypothalamus.[53] They still have the clock. The aplysia certainly has no cortex, yet it can accomplish all sorts of simple learning tasks. In fact, the analysis of intelligent action or learning abilities to a cellular level has become a reality through the study of the aplysia.[54]

The view that mind is the same as the brain has given way to philosophical functionalism, which does not identify thought with the brain: thought can be embodied in many kinds of substances (chapters 1 and 3). Some still believe[55] that thought is a secretion of the brain analogous to insulin being secreted by the pancreas. In this view, mind could never be simulated in artificial stuff, i.e., non-neural material. These are not ideological issues, but pragmatic ones, the resolution of which awaits the results of sustained inquiry that integrates our advances in neurobiology, physiology, psychology, philosophy, and artificial intelligence.[56]

Frame Problem

The neocortex is the organ that allows us to search for truth, inquire into the meaning of our lives, and create those warranted beliefs that we find meaningful. But it is hard enough to model intelligence in artificial systems (e.g., chips of silicon) for what brains do let alone to model rationality (chapter 2). It is, after all, hard enough to program machines to be smart in any of the ways that brains are. Wisdom is another question.

The frame problem has to do with modelling machines of artificial material to do what brains do with ease.[57] What hypotheses do they require? In other words, what knowledge must the machine of our making have to appear to solve problems the way brains do? The answers await further inquiry.

It is possible that theories unimaginable at this time might shed light on the frame problem, on our sense of ourselves and our experiences and their relationships to the brain, without reducing the experiences from our objective purview (chapter 1). This inquiry and the surprising results that will no doubt be revealed are part of the "adventures of ideas."[58]

Chapter 10

Possibilities and Constraints

Introduction

Possibilities for growth and inquiry abound and yet they seem elusive. In what sense do they exist? That they exist as possible states of affairs, as future occasions for actuality, is a natural answer. But it is a bit like saying that the difference between a possible and an actual state of affairs is that one is possible while the other is actual.

Whatever their reality, possibilities are nonetheless grasped, but certainly not all of them are; only some of them are expressed and become actual. In part, our cultural practices limit the kinds of possibilities considered. In part, the way our brains have evolved also limits the possibilities open to us. The possibilities our mind-brain imposes on us allow us to have a world in which to function; they constitute and regulate. When speaking of such possibilities, one refers to the design of the mind-brain.

Possibilities are not just nominal; they are not just fabrics of the mind. Nominalism is an impoverished philosophical pre-supposition. We have all had the experience of discovering that reality rejected some ideas in a rather brute manner. The world sets the stage for what is possible and for what is actual. As a *pragmatist*, I also need an idea of the world and of reality, as suggested in earlier chapters. This need is highly entrenched, with good reason, in our epistemological stances. The real is posited as a warranted hypothesis entrenched in a framework, though not free from skeptical concern.

It is suggested that imagination is the intermediate link between the possible and the actual. In many instances a possibility is imagined that may be realized. Without imaginative leaps, there is little hope for change and resurrection. One imagines what a just order would be like, and then one inquires and discourses about it. In this case, it is a possible state of affairs, under some historical condition.

The imagination is important in coming to know another being (chapter 1). To some extent the mental resonates with the real in the biological capacity to recognize the experiences of conspecifics and, at times, other animals. We imagine what the other is like. The actuality of the other may be grasped. Defining characteristics are hypothesized.

The imagination often gets things off the ground. Desire can stretch and help form new possibilities. This is one way that the imagination influences the possible. By imagining possibilities, resources are provided for determining actualities. The richness of the imagination provides the search for some of the resources, but not all; that is why its cultivation is important. But while the mind's capacity to imagine is essential, one should remember that the world is also an important factor in that it provides some of the resources for one to imagine possibilities and then instantiate them in actualities. Losing the world is falling into idiocy.

Possibilities, in the present context, are not ideals in Aristotle's sense but rather basic mental forms. The imagination works within these mental forms, creatively using them as resources. The desire to reach Aristotelian perfection in some of us is real and is a basic natural drive. But the focus here is on creatively using mental resources that are imaginatively tested against a world that initially selected for them in the evolutionary process. Our notion of freedom suggests that we creatively employ what we have, and not that we blindly try to reach some set determination of perfection.

Consider a dog named Red. Red, like most of us, has a set of behaviors (and experiences) that are to an extent always ready to go, ready to be triggered into action. They are mediated by representations (analogous to the mental representations discussed in chapter 8) in the mind, and they stand as possibilities in the repertoire of expressions of Red. A human companion pets and plays with Red regularly and knows him well enough to know how to trigger much of Red's repertoire. It is not difficult to discern his possibilities or to make them actual. Psychobiologists can uncover the design and engineering principles pre-supposed in order for Red to express what he does. The behavior is sometimes triggered because of a decisive factor embedded in Red's mind-brain; In-so-far as one believes that freedom is a natural biological property that speaks of degrees, one is inclined to attribute to Red some freedom. Our human biology, though more evolved, is related to Red's biology, as is our freedom. The difference between dogs and people is that people have more choice and more freedom—at least some do. We have more choice because of our mental resources. The behaviors are organized by possibilities of the mind-brain, for which there is finally a decisive factor before action; someone decides, at least some of the time. This is at the heart of inquiry. It is the issue of choice that is the essential factor in possibilities being expressed in actualities.

The hypothesis is that Red selects from possibilities and, by doing so, achieves some unity of being. To unify requires being decisive and active. The creative moment is in choosing and using the resources available. Because Red's repertoire is limited, so is his creativity. This is because Red does not have much from which to choose with which to be creative. Still there are imaginative components to Red's life that are expressed in the creative use of his strategies or forms of behaviors. The imaginative links the actual with the possible, in a sense analogous to the way the imaginative is the intermediary schema or connective thread in Kant between sense and the rules of thought.[1]

Choices are made among possibilities or else why speak of choice? The decision unifies the aggregates; possibilities are actualized and become embodied. The actuality is real and substantial. Insofar as one emerges from nature, freedom is to be construed as a matter of degree—not all or none. Despite this freedom, Red is often only an aggregate of parts, without a unified choice and sense of action, and is without freedom. But when Red decides, which he does on occasion, he achieves some unity; he selects among the possible.

There are varying degrees of this phenomenon that reflect evolutionary ascent and descent. Like Red the dog, humans are often aggregates; no unity dominates us, there is no choice and integrating creative event. One envisions dead habits instead. The person is lost in the habit, asleep. When one submerges oneself in habit one is more likely to be triggered like a tropic factor. Responsibility as an ontological human factor is lost; pushes and pulls predominate. But when persons creatively select from the possible, something very different emerges. Nausea is what some experience, awe is found by others, and depletion emerges for others. Some experience none of this, and some have a good time of it. Red has none of this. Ultimate moments for humans occur through choice and creativity. The rudiments of choice are tied to our biology and to that of animal life more generally. But for humans sometimes the choice is to limit our freedom, our options; Red probably does not do that.[2]

The point here is this: Decisions unify, they also make one bigger. They expand one's sense of being. This is where the possible and the actual meet: some sort of creative synthesis takes place. In contrast to the Aristotelian who posits form as actual and matter as potential, form is potential and the real is actual. What is posited as the possible in the present context is the presupposed mental fabric; the actual is the real world that selects the mental fabric. The event is not one of fulfilling a form, but of creatively using forms. It corresponds more to our sense of life.

Form and Knowledge

Inquiry is possible because of logic; thinking is possible because of logic. This is the logic of what Peirce called abduction, the logic of the genesis of ideas. It is the logic underlying our adaptations. That is, the formal properties of mind that set the possibilities for knowing. The mind constitutes, or imposes order; it is the condition for there being an intelligible order. The mind's categories are necessary in having a world at all, as well as having a self. Idealism and realism meet through real worlds being embedded in ideal minds that reach, on occassion, agreement through convergent tests about existence, despite the fact that agreements are never perfect and inquiry itself may never fully terminate.

Intelligibility, or problems solving, is an adaptive achievement of the mind (chapters 2 and 9), to which possibilities are presupposed mental functions. They are something like what Peirce meant by "frozen mind." The question for the epistemologist is: what kinds of mental competence does the creature presuppose in order to display the actualities it does?

The world matters in the formation of such minds. Our world has limited, or constrained, the kinds of ideas that we can generate. Here one looks to the ecological-cultural conditions to which minds adapt for guidance. These conditions also insured that we can hit on the right ideas; ideas are not always arbitrary, but are adaptive; they guide behavior. If the ideas are bad, they are rejected. Moreover, perhaps the constraints on our hypotheses are tied to our creative potential. The abductive and the creative are intimately linked: abductive moments are prototypical mental events—creatively generating ideas and inquiry and then testing them against the world (chapter 7).

In more contemporary terms, where no mental life is imposed, no problem solving is found. We talk about the constraints of cognitive organs, the limits of what they can do, how they operate, the strategies or hypotheses they employ. But we must consider not only the animal's mind, but also the world's impositions. The ecological-cultural niche is uncovered in the context of determining the behavioral options or strategies that can be employed. Without the notion of a world, the mind's possibilities lose all sensibility (e.g., light-dark-circadian cycles). The possibilities are often shared properties, and we can only exist embedded in a world.

Hypothesis Testing

A general feature of animals that inquire and learn is that of being a hypothesis tester. They discern first what it is they are faced with and then decide what is the appropriate response. They hypothesize and test. They alter their beliefs and actions if need be—at least ideally. The phenomenon is one of degrees. Genesis and feedback are pervasive and constantly overlie one another. Adaptation and success are features of the survivor. Approach and avoidance mechanisms organize the action (chapters 8 and 9). The hypotheses that work and resolve problems survive to become the habits for future engagements. As they become entrenched their novelty diminishes. The hypotheses, or beliefs, that orchestrate behavior are not altered until called into doubt, until some breakdown of a habit. Then the animal generates other hypotheses to test; with success there arrives the emergence of a new habit (chapters 2 and 6). The new habit, or entrenched belief, is instantiated in the brain and becomes a possible expression in the animal's repertoire.

Stated in the language of everyday life, at first the behavior feels lively and then it becomes routine. At first one is present; after awhile it is difficult to say where one is. These beliefs and actions through the course of time have become habitually applied and, as a result, have deadened somewhat. The liveliness is gone, but they are at the basis of organized action, they are part of the cognitive unconscious. But what is pervasive across all kinds of animal life is the capacity to test and change—through inquiry. The extent of this is contingent on the possibilities of expression open to the animal. But there is also some choice and creative use of one's mental resources. There is the enjoyment, or consummation (or not), of choice, inquiry, and action.

The mental has essentially to do with choice and check, with intelligent strategies and successful stays, with inquiry. Most essentially, the mental has to do with self-generative behavior and consummatory experience. Animals are essentially active and not passive, as the American pragmatic tradition so wonderfully understood (chapter 7). The active sense of mind-creating and hypothesizing is a pre-condition for achieving unity of being. The creative is tied to an active sense of mentation. If nature does not reject a hypothesis, it becomes an entrenched habit that eventually loses the essential abductive moment (the act of creating the hypothesis). In other words, the richness of the moment of creation is lost in its continued success. Routine and redundancy follow as stability is achieved. But the success is probably at sometime challenged; choice and hypothesis testing is renewed. In higher animals like ourselves, this moment is tied to reflection and understanding, and the whole show begins anew with new hypotheses to test. Thus while tropic factors are real, there is nonetheless activity in the animal; again the animal is not just passive, not just habitual. Since choice and check are at the heart of mental life, there is a common principle that can envision persons and ants as being natural elements and related to other biological kinds. Let us consider further the issue of mental constraints in a contemporary context.

Language Acquisition

There may be several linguistic constraints that are operative in language acquisition.[3] No language learning is possible without certain innate linguistic rules that set the conditions for the child learning the language of his or her culture. The linguistic rules are presupposed for the human language user. From a finite set of rules, or constraints, an infinite array of sentences can be generated. The finite set constrains, but richly so, allowing for creative linguistic expression. These linguistic rules are unconscious; we do not have privileged access to them.

Because almost all agree that there is no learning without innate rules, the question is one of degree. Empiricists say it is a small degree; rationalists say it is a large degree. Both agree that something innately given to the animal is presupposed, but differ on the scope of it. The job of the inquirer is to uncover them. In the case of language, one could not learn a language without presupposed linguistic rules. One is led with good reason to believe that a language-generating device is operative, that it may develop or mature, as do other biological organs over time, and that this maturation (though influenced by environmental contingencies) has built within it a rhythm of development endogenous to its nature. This also holds true for movements, birdsong, or cortical development.

The child acquires the language of his or her culture by generating hypotheses guided by universal syntactical constraints that serve the child in this acquisition. The child's creativity exploits the resources that stand as his or her possibilities. In the case of language, the syntactic constraints and the continuation of successful linguistic strategies are the resources. The problem for scientific inquiry is what presupposed, constitutive rules, syntactic constraints, or pragmatic strategies make possible creative language use.

Dietary Strategies

It is well warranted to assert that animals come into nature selectively prepared to learn some things quite easily.[4] The animals quickly learn to avoid noxious food; they select one food at a time, and determine the consequences. The learning takes place over a long temporal spread. This strategy mechanism designed specifically to solve food-related problems is important to an animal in nature. There are many other examples. Understanding intelligence, then, requires understanding the cognitive machinery that makes it possible, i.e., the strategies operative within the animal (chapter 2), to explore existing possibilities.

For example, when animals are rendered sodium deficient they search for salty sources—(salt licks). The knowledge is innate; the first time they are sodium deficient they ingest the salt immediately when exposed to it.[5] They recall where salt can be found when they are sodium deficient, despite the fact that they may have discovered the salt when they were sodium-replete. To the sodium-deficient animal, salt sources are noted and sought. This innate, specialized knowledge has been extended to other mineral deficiencies. Potassium and calcium deficient animals will also ingest salty sources. The very possibility of the sodium, potassium, or calcium deficient animal being able to solve its dietary needs requires the opening or horizon of salt-related events. The constraints of ingesting salty sources determine the ingestive responses. A "universe(s) of discourse" opens up. The creative use of the innate sodium appetite is extended to other minerals. In the world, salt licks are rich in other minerals besides sodium. But from the one innate appetite for salty tastes that results from sodium deficiency, the animal can resolve the other related mineral appetites in the strategy to ingest salty sources. The constraints make possible this creative moment.

The evolution of intelligence in this view is seen as the liberation of these strategies; specific adaptive achievements become more generally applied.[6] The use of these basic strategies in new domains speaks of the creative, the extension of possibilities provided by the animal's innately endowed resources. They foster inquiry.

Inquiry has revealed that the cognitive unconscious is a rich source—the predominant source—of our ideas. The cognitive unconscious is in varying degrees a highly specialized source so that the rules of linguistic use are distinguishable from those of reasoning about numbers, visual space perception, or dietary strategies. These cognitive organs are often highly modularized or specialized.[7]

Thinking Brains

The brain is largely designed for performing specific tasks (chapter 9). The design is often one of modularity; each neural system embodies specific design principles. The job of the neural scientist is to spell out how the different systems are designed and organized. Wiring diagrams are drawn, physiological and psychological mechanisms are uncovered, and the principles of the system are discerned, i.e., how it operates and the constraints on the system that make it possible. In thinking of how the system works, the neural scientist often considers the strategies employed by each system and whether different neural systems gain access to one another.

One attributes intelligence to such systems, neural or otherwise, when thinking about information processing, coding, transformations, and decision procedures. The design is again one of centrifugal control. And the cells in the retina, as well as those in the visual cortex, can be said to serve some function of mental activity. The mental activity is all theory-laden, from what the retina "sees" to what the visual cortices receive (chapter 3). The design is for reaching satisfaction.

The evolution of nervous systems suggests that increasing accessibility of one system to another may be at the basis of the rise of intelligent action, from specific to more general accessibility (chapters 2 and 9). The capacity to be responsive in a broad range of domains appears. The animals can then be said to know more and to do more because of such liberation. In some cases they can also be said to experience more. Such intelligent sentience is instantiated in neural design.

There is convergence of the mental and the physical. There is specialization, accessibility in a hierarchy of strategies, where decisive hypothesis testing takes place and where creative new strategies emerge. Each mind-brain system creates in a context because of constraints or possibilities that provide order. The more evolved the system the greater the capacity for creativity. Thus, each system decides and acts with varying degrees of freedom on the basis of its design—the constraints or order from which it works.

The Designer's Stance

In constructing a machine, one adopts the designer's stance. In the construction of artificial intelligent systems, one is placed in the position of having to design an apparatus to solve a problem or to perform some task. In the design of such systems, one has to think of strategies or what the system must know in order to solve the problem. One is put in a designer's, or creator's, position.

Our understanding of cognitive mechanisms—e.g., language-generating devices, visual systems, or the strategies of successful food selection—is further substantiated when our own design of an intelligent system can perform these functions. To understand a mental system and to give it psychological reality is, in part, to show that it is constitutive of an intelligent system of our own creation. This is a strong thesis for artificial simulation of cognitive capacities, and it is probably false. Yet it captures an intuition that has appeared in culture for several thousand years: to know something is to create something that displays the knowledge. The phrase "show me" is an old one. Without reducing all aspects of mind to bits of machinery, and so avoiding crude and false scientism, the study of artificial intelligence needs little defense. Simulation does teach us something about the design of systems and possibly the design of our own minds. Our own constructions, perhaps, may become known. So in understanding how knowledge is possible, one very important line of inquiry is the construction of intelligent systems. If the system is to perform, stated in this very general and abstract way, the constraints and strategies in terms of determining factors are at the heart of its design.

But we have not been very successful in producing sophisticated intelligent systems anything like that seen in animal life. This is the so called "frame problem" (chapter 9). Recall that the frame problem is in providing the knowledge requisite for intelligent behavior so that the thinking system can draw the right inferences in resolving problems in novel situations. Machines have not arrived yet. If a framework anything like our own or other animals' can be designed, then the designer's stance and real mentation would meet. Its possibility is in the distant future.

But, if in simulating the artificial, animal unity is achieved and a decision emerges to dominate and take hold of the many in a nontropic manner, then epistemology and metaphysics meet quite intimately. The epistemology is in uncovering the mental apparatus that organizes behavior and which gives meaning to the world. The metaphysics stipulates that at the heart of life are decisions that unify. Systematic psychobiology, in part, shows the natural relationships between the frameworks that animals work from and the decisions that are at the heart of their organic unity. For now, one knows that artificial simulation shares some of the design principles of biological systems and is compatible with the metaphysics of choice, action, and being.

Mentalism and Metaphysics

Theories in psychobiology are directed toward uncovering the operations of the mental apparatus in the context of real world selection pressures—cognition that is adapted to and in resonance, or harmony, with the environment. Conflicts for animals are resolved by intelligent actions. These actions provide the foundations for inquiry. The language of cognition is readily and intelligibly extended to biology,[8] and artificial thinking machines. The constrained systems, and decisions made through their use, constitute mental life.

The metaphysics is that, decisions predominate. This has been expressed by Sartre in the analysis of humans, by Whitehead in the analysis of everything.[9] The essential feature of an abductive mental event is a decision that integrates aggregate parts into a coherent action.

This is a metaphysics compatible with the contemporary turn towards cognitive theories. Decision making is revealed by the creative expression of thinking which is embedded in constraining factors yielding abductive moments of insight for inquiry.

The metaphysics goes a bit further. One speaks of determinate features,[10] or constraints or boundary conditions, in epistemological terms that set the possibilities for action. Resources are determinate recurring features, or the background conditions for subsequent occasions of pragmatic use. They are connected to real, often existential decisions.

The world to a mind therefore, comes designed in an order of determinate features. But without the creative, or abductive moments of inquiry, it would all be dead. Mind is absent when inert matter dominates. The regularity repeats itself, and deadness of habit rather than the achievement of the novel emerges. When alive, sentient, and thoughtful, the creative creature chooses from the past regularities and is geared toward a future of self-expression or decision. This is freedom with bonds, within environmental, psychobiological and cultural constraints.

The metaphysics and epistemology are of process, movement and action. The events are existential because they require decision; because they are tied to action they require pragmatism and resourcefulness. They are free yet constrained acts of self-determination, acts of genesis, or coming into being. The essential features are those of activity. At those moments, the past is captured by a decision. The creative power to unify, or choose not to, is directly related to the place the animal inhabits in the hierarchy of biological being.

But this metaphysical position is riddled with paradox. All metaphysical stances are mysterious. However, if one wants a metaphysics that justifies a concept of freedom as self-determination (or imaginative decision), constrained by determinate factors (background data), and expressed in acts of genesis, this one has some warrant. The metaphysics is also compatible with an epistemology that envisions mentation as decisions within constraints; mind as the creative tester in many cases producing a brilliant survivor or thriver. Constraints and the world, the determining or limiting factors, set the possibilities. Essential features, in contrast to determinate features, are the acts of abductive moments of bringing something into being through decision, action, and inquiry. The world is constantly being rejuvenated through decision, action and inquiry.

As knowers, we often seek unity. One of the messages of the modern age is that if the "world(s)" we live in are radically incongruous, are not unifiable, then the endeavor of looking to unify is useless. In fact, discontinuity is also at times essential for discovery, inquiry and advance. We can choose non-unity, and impose our own constraints on the choices we make. That is we can reduce not only our sense of unity, but our choices. Perhaps, this event is only true of humans. There is no perfect point of stasis. What one needs is principled fluidity. The world changes and one needs to be responsive to these changes. The inquirer, therefore, lives in a state of principled fluidity; he or she is open to change. Thus, there is no unity, and often conflicting and disparate selves at many moments. But if one strives to provide some coherence to the many frameworks we inhabit, then vague hypotheses are inevitable and possibly desirable.[11] The advance consists in connecting the disparity or coping with it. Unification of our conceptual world is a basic goal, as well as an advance in our sense of experience. But reaching maturity is living with those many instances of life where things do not come together, and still maintaining one's sense of integrity and connectedness and concern for others—whether or not they speak our language or agree with our views. There is no permanent resting place, just ephemeral moments of peace of an evolving inquirer.

Freedom is therefore within form. The form stands as possibilities, as constraints in epistemological terms, or determinate features in metaphysical terms. There are many orders of determinate features. The degree of determinateness is contingent on the range of possibilities and past creative abductive syntheses. The more free, the greater the range. The denial of this in humans is where one can speak of Sartrian "bad faith" since freedom and choice are at the heart of being. But the extent to which a person integrates is always difficult to discern, making the problem of attributing responsibility greater. But the existentialist's fear, or nausea, is a self-imposed limitation resulting from a concept of radical freedom. Freedom, however, is constrained; this corresponds with our sense of things, with our "funded knowledge." In other words, there is no such thing as radical freedom. Our psychobiological makeup, cultural institutions, our aggregate selves constrain our choices. Still, a splendid array of choices are often possible when there is not madness, delusion or narcissism. Human talent for creative problem-solving, and the human capacity for principled action, fuse together to portray a person not mired by freedom, but empowered through inquiry. Perhaps, a realized human is a good inquirer.

Conclusion

Each chapter has highlighted several threads of human experience. In each, "inquiry" is shown to be central to coming to terms with what we experience and with going on to experience new things. The sense of being in the world conveyed was one of being an active agent; our problem solving proclivities can be brought to bear on matters of great importance to ourselves; the pursuit of wisdom and the good life. While our theories determine our various pursuits, a strong conception of the real predominates; good *pragmatists* almost always have a sense of the real. Besides hypotheses are rejected daily. And so one can be reminded that our theories are not just make believe. And, moreover, they do not just exist in a vacuum; the dilemmas of life require the strategies of good sense. They require good hypotheses, inquiry and modes of engagement. Our survival depends on them.

Our survival also depends on the cultivation of the public; the sphere in which we move around: the social bonds of consequences. With the loss of the public, there looms the danger of the fall into idiocy; the privation of being that robs one of the ability to function in the world. It is after all our social intelligence that can move one to bond favorably and positively with others. Perhaps there will always be the seduction of comfort and the covering up of one's individual responsibility while clothing it with the bad faith of self deception.

We are human and prone to all sorts of maladies, some of which are not of our own doing. Madness, and normal psychopathologies, are constant reminders. They have consequences; they have determinate results on what one is and how one experiences the world. Still one admires those who rise to the extreme and overcome the frailities of human encounter. It remains one of the great wonders of human experience. At its heart there is the steadfast of ingenuity and inquiry coupled with an unyielding faith in prospect and promise. Amidst the fallen cries there is the wonder of human dignity and the march forward.

The cultural march is presupposed by an evolutionary history. Our evolutionary history is one of an advanced mammalian brain; it evolved principally for problem solving, but pleasures of the senses coupled with cognitive capacities insured motivational pulls; one is the achievement of the beautiful and the sublime. Discovery, learning and inquiry are fundamental events in the process. This is the biological context. The cultural one is the rise foward, the expression of leadership and the realistic assessment of the political, in all activities including those of inquiry.

An inquiring mind at its best is neither scientistic nor fatalistic; realism tempered with hope is what predominates. While inquiry will not solve all of life's dilemmas, we also need love and good fortune; the pursuit of inquiry is the river that we swim, ride and channel, while we are reminded of the dangers and the storms that will emerge.

Notes

Introduction

1. See, for example, J. Dewey's *Human Nature and Conduct* (orig. 1922, 1950, Random House).

2. J. Sartre's *Being and Nothingness* (orig. 1943, 1956, Washington Square Press) would be a good example.

3. S. Kierkegaard. *Concluding Unscientific Postscript* (orig. 1848, 1941, transl. D. Swenson, Princeton Univ. Press).

4. This is not true of course for William James. See, for example, *Varieties of Religious Experience* (orig. 1902, 1974, Collier MacMillan Publ. Co.).

5. See, for example, R. Rorty's *Consequences of Pragmatism* (1982, Univ. of Minnesota Press), *Philosophical Papers* (1991, Volumes I & II, Cambridge Univ. Press).

6. See J. Smith's *The Spirit of American Philosophy* (1963, Oxford Univ. Press).

7. M. White. *Positivism and Pragmatism: Toward a Reunion in Philosophy* (1956, Harvard Univ. Press).

8. See, for example, W. Quine's *The Ways of Paradox and Other Essays* (1976, Harvard Univ. Press).

9. See C. Lewis' *Mind and the World Order* (orig. 1929, 1956, Dover Press.

10. See K. Apel's *Understanding and Explanation* (1984, MIT Press).

Chapter 1

1. In modern form this is represented by A. Ayer's *Language, Truth and Logic* (orig. 1936, 1952, Dover). Or see R. Carnap's *The Logical Structure of the World* (orig. 1928, 1969, Univ. of California Press).

2. E. Husserl's *Cartesian Mediation* (orig. 1929, 1973, The Hague).

3. L. Wittgenstein's *Philosophical Investigations* (1952, MacMillan & Co.).

4. See D. Dennett's *Brainstorms* (1978, Bradford Books).

5. J. Sabini & M. Silver. *Moralities of Everyday Life* (1982, Oxford Press).

6. S. Delza's *Tai-Chi-Chuan* (orig. 1961, 1985, SUNY Press).

7. See, for example, N. Chomsky's *Aspects of a Theory of Syntax* (1965, MIT Press).

8. J. Fodor, "The Mind-Body Problem" (1981, *Scientific American*).

9. J. Schulkin, *Sodium Hunger* (1991, Cambridge Univ. Press).

10. T. Nagel's *Mortal Questions* (1979, Cambridge Univ. Press 168, 169).

11. See D. Griffin's *Listening in the Dark* (1974, Dover).

12. Following R. Rorty, see Paul Churchland's *Scientific Realism and the Plasticity of Mind* (1979, Cambridge Univ. Press) for a recent example of this.

13. See R. Rorty's *Contingency, Irony and Solidarity* (1979, Cambridge Univ. Press).

14. See W. James' *The Varieties of Religious Experience* (orig. 1902, 1974, MacMillan Publ. Co.)

15. C. Turnball *"East African Safari"* (1981, Natural History).

16. From the *N.Y. Times*, 1981.

17. See, for example, G. Schaller's *The Year of the Gorilla* (1964, Univ. of Chicago Press).

18. See, for example, S. Freud's *A General Introduction to Psychoanalysis* (orig. 1924, 1960, Wash Sq. Press), Ruth Benedict's *Patterns of Culture* (orig. 1934, 1953, Mentor Books), and M. Merleau-Ponty's *The Primacy of Perception* (1964, Northwestern Univ. Press).

19. See J. Dewey's *Experience and Nature* (orig. 1925, 1989, Open Court).

Chapter 2

1. See, for example, T. Ricketts' *Rationality, Translation, and Epistemology Naturalized* (1982, *Journal of Philosophy*).

2. A. Whitehead's *The Function of Reason* (1929, Princeton Univ. Press).

3. See, for example, R. Neville's *The Cosmology of Freedom* (1974, Yale University Press).

4. See, for example, I. Hacking's *Logic of Statistical Inference* (1965, Cambridge University Press).

5. A. Dickinson's *Contemporary Animal Learning Theory* (1980, Cambridge Univ. Press) or D. Kahneman and A. Tversky's *On The Psychology of Prediction* (1973, *Psychological review*).

6. See R. Rescorla's *Information Variables in Pavlovian Conditioning* (1972, Academic Press) or J. Smith's *Behavior of Communications* (1977, Harvard Univ. Press).

7. P. Rozin, *Evolution of Intelligence: Access to the Cognitive Unconscious* (1976, Academic Press).

8. See Jon Elster's *Sour Grapes* (1983, Cambridge Univ. Press).

9. H. Simon, *Sciences of the Artificial* (1967, MIT Press).

10. See, for example, T. Ricketts' *The Tractatus and the Logocentric Predicament* (1985, Nous).

11. J. Fodor, *The Language of Thought* (1979, Harvard Univ. Press).

12. J. Baron, *Rationality and Intelligence* (1985, Cambridge Univ. Press).

13. See J. Dewey's *How We Think* (1910, Heath & Co.).

14. J. Elster, *Ulysses and the Sirens* (1979, Cambridge Univ. Press).

15. See, for example, J. Dewey's *Human Nature and Conduct* (orig. 1922, 1950, Random House).

16. See P. Grice, "Meaning" (1957, *Philosophical Review*).

17. C. Woodruff and D. Premack, "Intentional Communication in the Chimpanzee: The Development of Perception" (1979, *Cognition*).

18. Outside pragmatism, see for example, H. Arendt's *The Human Condition* (1958, Univ. of Chicago Press), or H. Gadamer's *Truth and Method* (orig. 1960, 1985, Crossroad Publ. Co.).

19. J. Dewey, *Experience and Education* (1952, Collier Book).

20. See, for example, J. Habermas' *Theory and Practice* (1973, Beacon Press) and *Legitimation Crisis* (1975, Beacon Press).

21. J. Rawls, *A Theory of Justice* (1971, Harvard Univ. Press).

22. See, for example, R. Neville's *Axiology of Thinking* (1983, SUNY Press).

Chapter 3

1. See, for example, B. Spinoza *On the Improvements of Understanding* (orig. 1665, 1955, Dover Press).

2. I. Kant, *Critique of Pure Reason* (orig. 1787, 1965, St. Martin's Press).

3. See R. Descartes' *Discourse on Method and Mediations* (orig. 1663, 1967, Bobbs-Merrill Co.).

4. See J. Sartre's *Being and Nothingness* (orig. 1943, 1956, Wash. Sq. Press).

5. Kant, ibid.

6. See, for example, L. Wittgenstein's *Philosophical Investigations* (orig. 1953, 1968, MacMillan Publishing Co.).

7. R. Gallistel's *Organization of Action* makes a good case for this (1980, Erlbaum Press).

8. See G. Rey's *Functionalism and the Emotions* (1980, Univ. of Calif. Press).

9. C. Darwin's classic *The Expression of the Emotions in Man and Animals* (orig. 1879, 1965, Univ. of Chicago Press).

10. See W. Sellars' *Science Perception and Reality* (1962, Rutledge and Kegan) and *Science and Metaphysics* (1968, Humanities Press).

11. See, for example, Kant, Ibid., and C. I. Lewis, *Mind and the World Order* (orig. 1929, 1956, Dover Press).

12. See D. Marr's *Vision* (1982, W. H. Freeman & Co).

13. J. J. Gibson. *The Senses Considered as Perceptual Systems* (1966, Houghton-Mifflin).

14. W. V. Quine. *The Ways of Paradox and Other Essays* (1976, Harvard Univ. Press).

15. This point is made by many people in addition to the classical pragmatists, see, e.g., N. Hanson's *Patterns of Discovery* (orig. 1958, 1972, Cambridge Univ. Press), P. Heelan, *Space Perception and the Philosophy of Science* (1983, Univ. of California Press).

16. See N. Goodman's *Fact, Fiction and Forecast* (orig. 1955, 1973, Bobbs-Merrill & Co.).

17. See J. Parrott and J. Schulkin, *Neuropsychology and the Cognitive Nature of Emotions* (1992, Cognition and Emotion).

18. See A. Beck's *Depression* (orig. 1967, 1978, Univ. of Penn. Press).

19. See L. Wittgenstein's *Philosophical Investigations* (orig. 1953, 1968, MacMillan Publ. Co.) or L. Vygotsky's *Thought & Language* (orig. 1936, 1979, MIT Press).

20. See R. DeRubeis and A. Beck, *Cognitive Therapy* (1988, Guilford Press).

21. J. Fodor, *The Modularity of Mind* (1982, MIT Press).

22. J. Sartre, *Being and Nothingness* (orig. 1943, 1956, Wash. Sq. Press).

23. See C. Peirce's "How to Make our Ideas Clear" (1878, *Popular Science Monthly*), or T. Nagel's *The View from Nowhere* (1986, Oxford Univ. Press).

Chapter 4

1. See T. Des Pres' *The Survivor* (1977, Pocket Books, p. 47).

2. See E. Wilson's book *Sociobiology* (1975, Harvard University Press) for what I have in mind.

3. See A. Camus' *The Plague* (1972, Vintage Press).

4. Ibid., p. 71.

5. Ibid., p. 174.

6. From E. Goffman's *Asylums* (1961, Anchor Books, p. 188).

7. B. Bettleheim, *Surviving and other Essays* (1980, Vintage Press, p. 76–77).

8. See H. Arendt's brilliant and courageous books *Eichman in Jerusalem* (1963, Viking Press).

9. See L. Baker's *Days of Sorrow and Pain* (1978, Oxford University Press).

10. See S. Milgram's *Obedience to Authority* (1975, Harper Press).

11. Arendt, ibid., p. 54.

12. See Adorno, et al., *The Authoritarian Personality* (1966, Harper and Row), and E. Fromm's *Escape from Freedom* (1941, Holt, Rinehart, and Winston).

13. Arendt, ibid., p. 30.

14. See G. Sereny's *Into that Darkness: An Examination of Conscience* (1983, Vantage Books).

15. See R. Rorty's book *Contingency, Irony, and Solidarity* (1989, Cambridge University Press) for an erudite justification of this position.

16. Milgram, ibid., p. 6.

17. See J. Gray's *The Warriors: Reflections on Men in Battle* (1967, Harper Torch Books).

18. Gray, ibid., p. 8.

19. Gray, ibid., p. 46.

20. See W. Laqueur's *The Terrible Secret* (1982, Penguin Press).

21. J. Sabini and M. Silver's *Moralities of Everyday Life* (1982, Oxford Press), makes this point elegantly.

22. Sabini and Silver, ibid.

23. See S. Lasch's *The Minimal Self* (1984, Norton Press).

24. See J. Korczak's *Ghetto Diary* (1978, Holocaust Library).

25. See T. Hobbes' *Leviathan* (orig. 1651, 1958, Bobbs Merrill & Co.).

26. J. Rousseau's *A Discourse on Inequality* (orig. 1755, 1984, Penguin Press).

27. See E. Weisel's *Night* (1982, Bartram Books, p. 32).

Chapter 5

1. See, for example, T. Nagel's *The View From Nowhere* (1986, Oxford Press).

2. R. Neville, *Soldier, Sage, and Saint* (1978, Fordham Univ. Press).

3. M. Mahler, F. Pine, and A. Bergman, *The Psychological Birth of the Human Infant* (1975, Basic Books).

4. H. Kohut, *Self Psychology and the Humanities* (1985, Norton Press).

5. D. Winnicott, *The Child, the Family and the Outside World* (orig. 1957, 1987, Addison Publ. Co.).

6. R. White, "Motivation Reconsidered: The Concept of Competence" (1959, *Psychological Review*).

7. J. Dewey, *Human Nature and Conduct* (1922, Random House).

8. H. Fingarette, *The Self in Transformation* (1965, Harper Books).

9. See W. James' *Principles of Psychology* (orig. 1890, 1950, Dover Press) or G. Mead, *Mind, Self & Society* (1934, Univ. of Chicago Press).

10. See, for example, H. Kohut's *Self Psychology and the Humanities* (1985, Norton Press).

11. E. Fromm, D. Suzuki & R. DeMartino, *Zen Buddhism & Psychoanalysis* (1960, Harper and Row).

12. D. Winnicott, *The Child, the Family and the Outside World* (orig. 1957, 1987, Addison-Wesley Publ. Co.).

13. M. Klein, *Psychoanalysis of Children* (orig. 1932, 1975, Delta Publishers).

14. Kohut, ibid.

15. W. Fairbairn, "Synopsis of an Object Relations Theory of Personality" (1963, *Int. J. of Psychoanalysis*).

16. A. Miller, *The Drama of the Gifted Child* (1981, trans. R. Ward, Basic Books).

17. C. Lasch, *The Minimal Self* (1984, Norton Press).

18. James, ibid.

19. V. Frankl, *Psychotherapy and Existentialism* (1967, Wash. Sq. Press).

20. A. Schopenhauer, *On the Freedom of the Will* (orig. 1839, 1985, Basil Blackwell) F. Schiller, *On the Aesthetic Education of Man* (orig. 1795, 1980, Ungar Publ.), F. Nietzche, *Beyond Good & Evil* (orig. 1886, 1966, Vantage Books).

21. I. Kant, *Critique of Practical Reason* (orig. 1788, 1956, Bobbs-Merrill Co.).

22. J. Sabini & M. Silver, *Moralities of Everyday Life* (1982, Oxford Univ. Press).

23. W. Fairbairn, *Synopsis of an Object-Relations Theory of Personality* (1963, *Int. J. of Psychoanalysis*).

24. Kohut, ibid.

25. Kohut, ibid., p. 46.

26. S. Freud, *A General Introduction to Psychoanalysis* (orig. 1924, 1960, Wash. Sq. Press).

27. Klein, ibid.

28. W. James, *The Will to Believe, Human Immortality and Other Essays in Popular Philosophy* (orig. 1896, 1956 Dover Press).

29. See, for example, Freud ibid., and R. Goy & B. McEwen *Sexual Differentiation of the Brain* (1980, MIT Press).

30. H. Frankfurt, *The Importance of What We Care About* (1988, Cambridge Univ. Press).

31. B. Spinoza, *On the Improvement of the Understanding* (orig. 1688, 1955, Dover Press, p. 271).

32. See G. Vico's *On the Most Ancient Wisdom of Italians* (orig. 1910, 1988, Cornell Univ. Press).

Chapter 6

1. See, for example, C. S. Peirce's "The Fixation of Belief" (1877, *Popular Sci. Mo.*).

2. J. Dewey, *Democracy and Education* (1916, Univ. of Chicago) or *Experience and Education* (1952, Collier Books).

3. T. Kuhn, *The Structure of Scientific Revolution* (1962, Univ. of Chicago Press).

4. See M. Weber's *Social and Economic Organization* (1947, Oxford Univ. Press).

5. A. Whitehead, *Adventures of Ideas* (orig. 1933, 1967, Free Press).

6. E. Fromm, *Escape from Freedom* (1941, Holt, Rinehart).

7. J. Dewey, *The Quest for Certainty* (1929, G.P. Putnam & Sons).

8. See R. Neville's *The Puritan Smile* (1987, SUNY Press).

9. L. Feuerbach's *Principles of the Philosophy of the Future* (orig. 1843, 1986, Hackett Publishing Company, p. 71).

10. See, for example, S. Freud's *Civilization and its Discontents* (orig. 1930, 1962, Norton Press).

11. See A. Whitehead's *Adventures of Ideas* (orig. 1933, 1967, Free Press).

Chapter 7

1. See, for example, reviews by H. Schneider, *A History of American Philosophy* (orig. 1946, 1963, Columbia Univ. Press) and E. Flower & M. Murphy, *A History of Philosophy in America*, Vol. I & II (1977, Capricorn Books).

2. Schneider, ibid.

3. See, for example, *Thomas Jefferson on Democracy* (1939, Mentor Books).

4. See, for example, R. Emerson's *A Modern Anthology* (1958, Dell Press) or *Great Short Works of Thoreau* (1971, Harper & Row).

5. See W. James' *Principles of Psychology* (orig. 1890, 1950, Dover Publications).

6. W. James, *The Will to Believe, Human Immortality and Other Essays in Popular Philosophy* (orig. 1896, 1956, Dover Press).

7. I. Kant, *Critique of Pure Reason* (orig. 1787, 1965, St. Martin's Press).

8. A. Whitehead, *Symbolism* (orig. 1927, 1952, MacMillian Co.).

9. C. Darwin, *The Expression of the Emotions in Man and Animals* (orig. 1879, 1965, Univ. of Chicago Press).

10. See *Collected Works of C. S. Peirce* Vol. I–VI (1932–1935, Harvard Univ. Press).

11. J. Piaget, *The Child & Reality* (1972, Penguin Books).

12. C. Peirce, "Logical Machines" (1887, *Am. J. of Psychology*, p. 168).

13. For example, see J. Fodor's *The Language of Thought* (1979, Harvard Univ. Press).

14. N. Chomsky, *Language & Mind* (1972, Harcourt Brace Jovanovich).

15. A. Dickinson, *Animal Learning Theory* (1980, Cambridge Univ. Press).

16. See C. Morris' *Foundations of the Theory of Signs* (1938, Univ. of Chicago).

17. See C. Wright, *Philosophical Writings* (1958, Liberal Arts Press).

18. See, for example, J. Dewey, *The Influence of Darwin on Philosophy* (orig. 1910, 1965, Indiana Univ. Press).

19. See, for example, J. Dewey, *Experience and Nature* (orig. 1929, 1989, Open Court).

20. See J. Dewey's *Logic: The Theory of Inquiry* (1938, Holt, Rinehart).

21. See, for example, J. Dewey's *Democracy & Education* (1916, Univ. of Chicago Press) or G. Mead's *Mind, Self & Society* (1934, Univ. of Chicago Press).

22. A. de Tocqueville, *A Democracy in America* (orig. 1848, 1945, Vintage Books).

23. P. Weiner, *Evolution and the Founders of Pragmatism* (1949, Harvard Univ. Press).

24. See R. Neville's *Recovery of the Measure* (1989, SUNY Press).

25. See J. Smith's *Themes in American Philosophy* (1970, Harper & Row) or *Purpose and Thought* (1978, Yale University Press).

26. See, for example, M. Mead's *Coming of Age in Samoa* (1928, William Morrow, D.C.).

27. J. Barzun, *The Culture We Deserve* (1989, Wesleyan Univ. Press).

28. C. Herrick, *The Brains of Rats and Men* (orig. 1926, 1967, Hafner Publishers, p. 20).

29. See B. Franklin's *Essays, Articles, Bagatelles, and Letters, Poor Richards Almanac, Autobiography* (1987, Library of America).

30. See R. Bernstein's *Praxis and Action* (1971, Univ. of Pennsylvania Press).

Chapter 8

1. C. Sachs, *World History of Dance* (1937, Norton Press, p. 139).

2. S. Langer, *Problems of Art* (1957, Charles Scribner and Sons, p. 12).

3. I. Kant, *Critique of Judgement* (orig. 1790, 1951, Hafner Press, p. 108).

4. Ibid., p. 85.

5. See M. Mahler, F. Pine, and A. Bergman's *The Psychological Birth of the Human Infant* (1975, Basic Books).

6. W. Kohler, *The Mentality of Apes* (1925, Routledge and Kegan Paul, p. 314).

7. A. Armstrong, *Bird Display and Behavior* (1965, Dover Press, p. 207).

8. D. Premack, Personal Communication.

9. See L. Von-Frish's brilliant study *The Dancing Bees* (1953, Harvest/HBJ Press).

10. See, for example, *The Neurobiology of Motivation and Reward* by J. Stellar and E. Stellar (1985, Springer-Verlag).

11. See T. Schneirla's *An Evolutionary and Development Theory of Biphasic Approach and Withdrawal* (1959, Freedman & Co.).

12. See, for example, J. Dewey's *Logic: The Theory of Inquiry* (1938, Holt Rinehart).

13. C. Hartshorne's *Some Biological Principles Application to Song Behavior* (1958, Wilson Bull).

14. See F. Nottebohn's *Brain Pathways for Vocal Learning in Birds* (1980, Academic Press).

15. See, for example, M. Merleau-Ponty's *The Primacy of Perception* (1964, Northwestern University) or A. Whitehead's *Symbolism* (origin. 1927, 1953, MacMillan Company).

16. See K. Mason's *Dance Therapy* (1974, A. A. for Health, Educ. and Recreation).

17. See P. Rozin's *The Evolution of Intelligence: Access to the Cognitive Unconscious* (1976, Academic Press).

18. J. Sartre, *Being and Nothingness* (origin. 1943, 1956, Washington Sq. Press).

19. See H. Feigl's *The Mental and the Physical* (1967, Univ. of Minn. Press).

20. See S. Delza's *Tai-Chi-Chuan* (orig. 1961, 1985, SUNY Press).

21. See *Ethical Writings of Maimonides* (1975, Dover Press).

Chapter 9

1. N. Eldridge, *Time Frames* (1985, Simon & Schuster).

2. See, for example, J. Fodor's *The Modularity of Mind* (1985, MIT Press).

3. See review by R. Young, *Mind, Brain and Adaptation* (1970, Oxford Press).

4. A. Brodal, *Neurological Anatomy* (1981, Oxford Univ. Press).

5. K. Lashley, *Brain Mechanisms and Intelligence* (1929, Univ. of Chicago Press).

6. See N. Geschwind's *Selected Papers on Language and the Brain* (1974, D. Reidel Publishing).

7. H. Jackson, *Evolution and Dissolution of the Nervous System* (orig. 1884, 1958, London Stapples Press).

8. See L. Squire's *Memory and Brain* (1987, Oxford Univ. Press).

9. Jackson, ibid., p. 41.

10. P. Bard, Central Nervous Mechanisms for Emotional Behavior Patterns in Animals (1939, *Research in Nervous & Mental Disease*).

11. Bard, ibid., p. 216.

12. R. Norgren and H. Grill, *Brainstem Control of Ingestive Behavior* (1982, Springer-Verlag).

13. Bard, ibid., p. 316.

14. E. Evarts, "Changing Conceptions of the Central Nervous System" (1975, *Canadian J. of Physiol.*).

15. P. Teitelbaum, *Physiological Psychology* (1967, Prentice-Hall).

16. J. Steiner, "*The Gastro-Facial Response: Observations on Normal and Anencephalic Newborn Infants*" (1973, U.S. Gov't. Printing Office).

17. W. James, *Principles of Psychology* (orig. 1980, 1950, Dover Press).

18. See C. Gallistel's *The Organization of Action* (1980, Erlbaum Press).

19. See C. Gallistel's *The Organization of Learning* (1990, MIT Press).

20. C. Herrick, *Neurological Foundations of Animal Behavior* (1924, Hafner Publishing).

21. F. Goltz, *On the Functions of the Hemispheres* (orig. 1888, 1978, McGraw-Hill).

22. Lashley, ibid.

23. N. MacKintosh, "A Theory of Attention" (1975), *Psychological Review.*

24. See, for example, E. Krieckhaus and C. Erikson, "A Study of Awareness and Its Effect on Learning and Generalization" (1960, *J. of Personality*).

25. K. Goldstein, "The Mental Changes Due to Frontal Lobe Damage" (1944, *J. of Psychology*).

26. James, ibid., p. 79.

27. See, for example, I. Pavlov's *Conditioned Reflexes* (1927, Dover Press).

28. J. Loeb, *Comparative Physiology of the Brain* (orig. 1900, 1973, Dover Press, p. 142).

29. Gallistel, ibid.

30. A. Dickinson, *Contemporary Animal Learning Theory* (1980, Cambridge Univ. Press).

31. Lashley, ibid.

32. J. McCelland and D. Rumelhart, *Parallel Distribution Processing* (1986, MIT Press).

33. Fodor, ibid.

34. Gallistel, ibid.

35. Brodal, ibid.

36. N. Chomsky, *Language and Mind* (1972, Harcourt Brace Jovanovich).

37. Geshwind, ibid.

38. H. Jerrison, *Evolution of the Brain and Intelligence* (1973, Academic Press, p. 9).

39. F. Nottebohm, *Brain Pathways and Vocal Learning in Birds* (1980, Academic Press).

40. Herrick, ibid.

41. D. Hebb, *The Organization of Behavior: A Neuropsychological Theory* (1949, John Wiley & Sons).

42. Brodal, ibid.

43. A. Epstein, *Instinct and Motivation as Explanations of Complex Behavior* (1982, Springer-Verlag).

44. P. MacLean, "Psychosomatic Disease and the Visceral Brain" (1949, *Psychosomatic Medicine*).

45. J. Papez, "A Proposed Mechanism of Emotion" (1937, *Archives of Neurology and Psychiatry*).

46. See, for example, R. Goy and B. McEwen's *Sexual Differentiation of the Brain* (1980, MIT Press).

47. M. Mishkin, B. Malamut, and J. Bahevalism, *"Memories and Habits"* (1984, Guilford Press).

48. See, for example, Evarts, ibid.

49. James, ibid.

50. H. Simon, *The Sciences of the Artificial* (1967, MIT Press, p. 205).

51. J. McCelland and D. Rumelhart, *Parallel Distributed Processing* (1986, MIT Press).

52. See, for example, H. Jennings' *Behavior of the Lower Organism* (orig. 1905, 1962, Indiana Univ. Press).

53. A. Rosenwasser and N. Adler, "Structure and Function in Circadian Timing Systems: Evidence for Multiplied Coupled Circadian Oxillators" (1986, *Neuroscience and Biobehavioral Reviews*).

54. E. Kandel, *Cellular Basis of Behavior* (1976, W. H. Freeman & Co.).

55. J. Searle, *Minds, Brain & Science* (1986, Harvard Univ. Press).

56. D. Marr, *Vision* (1982, W, H. & Freeman & Co.) or *Artificial Intelligence* (1981, MIT Press).

57. D. Dennett, *"Cognitive Wheels: The Frame Problem of AI"* (1984, Cambridge Univ. Press).

58. A. Whitehead, *Adventures of Ideas* (orig. 1933, 1967, Free Press).

Chapter 10

1. I. Kant discusses this in the *Critique of Pure Reason* (orig. 1787, 1965 McMillan & Co.).

2. See J. Elster's *Ulysses and the Sirens* (1979, Cambridge University Press), for an excellent discussion of how we limit our choices.

3. N. Chomsky makes this point in a number of places, but see his *Language and Mind* (1972, Harcourt Brace Jovanovich).

4. See P. Rozin and J. Schulkin in *Food Selection* (1990, Academic Press) for a more detailed discussion of these issues.

5. Two books document these facts in great detail: my own, *Sodium Hunger* (1991, Cambridge Univ. Press), and D. Denton's *The Hunger for Sodium* (1982, Springer-Verlag).

6. P. Rozin, *"Evolution of Intelligence: Access to the Cognitive Unconscious"* (1976, Academic Press).

7. See Jerry Fodor's succinct statement of this in his book *The Modularity of Mind* (1983, MIT Press).

8. N. Geschwind's *Neurological Knowledge and Complex Behaviors* (1980, Cognitive Science) makes this point clearly.

9. See J. Sartre's *Being and Nothingness* (orig. 1943, 1956, Washington Square Press) and A. N. Whitehead's *Process and Reality* (orig. 1929, 1979, MacMillan).

10. These points are made elegantly by P. Weiss' *Modes of Being* (1958, Southern Illinois University Press) and R. Neville's *The Cosmology of Freedom* (1974, Yale University Press).

11. Following points made by C. Peirce, see R. Neville's *Axiology of Thinking* (1983, SUNY Press).

Bibliography

Abeles, M. and Goldstein, M. H., Jr. (1970). "Functional architecture in cat primary auditory cortex. Columnar organization and organization according to depth." *Journal of Neurophysiology*, 33: 172-187.

Adorno, T. W., Frenkel-Brunswick, E. F., Levinson, D. J. and Sandford, R. N. (1966). *The Authoritarian Personality.* New York: Harper and Row.

Anscombe, G. E. M. (1963). *Intention.* Ithaca, New York: Cornell University Press.

Apel, K. O. (1981). *Charles Saunders Peirce: From Pragmatism to Pragmaticism* (transl. by J. M. Krois). Amherst: Univ. of Mass.

Apel, K. O. (1984). *Understanding and Explanation* (transl. by G. Warnke). Cambridge: MIT Press.

Aquinas, Thomas St. (1266–1268, 1988). *On Politics and Ethics* (trans. and edited by P. E. Sigmund), New York: W. W. Norton & Co.

Arendt, H. (1958). *The Human Condition.* Chicago: University of Chicago Press.

Arendt, H. (1963). *Eichman in Jerusalem.* New York: Viking Press.

Aristotle (1968). *DeAnima* (trans. by D. W. Hamlyn). Clarendon Aristotle Series, J. L. Ackrill (General editor). Oxford: Clarendon Press.

Aristotle (1968) *Metaphysics* (transl. by R. Hope). Michigan: University of Michigan Press.

Aristotle (1974). *Ethics* (transl. by J. A. K. Thompson). Baltimore: Penguin Press.

Armstrong, A. (1965). *Bird Display and Behavior.* New York: Dover Publication.

Augustine, St. (1949). *The Confessions of Saint Augustine* (transl. by E. B. Pusey). New York: Random House.

Austin, J. (1970). *Philosophical Papers.* Oxford: Oxford University Press.

Ayer, A. J. (1936, 1952). *Language, Truth and Logic.* New York: Dover Publications.

Bacon, F. (this edition, 1887). *Novum Organum.* Oxford: Oxford University Press.

Baker, L. (1978). *Days of Sorrow and Pain.* New York: Oxford University Press.

Bard, P. (1939). "Central nervous mechanisms for emotional behavior patterns in animals." *Research in Nervous and Mental Disease,* XXIX, 190–218.

Bard, P. and Rioch, D. Mc. (1937). "A study of four cats deprived of neocortex and additional portions of the forebrain." *Johns Hopkins Medical Journal,* 60: 73–153.

Baron, J. (1985). *Rationality and Intelligence.* Cambridge: Cambridge University Press.

Barzun, J. (1989). *The Culture We Deserve.* Connecticut: Wesleyan University Press.

Bechterev, V. M. (1917). *General Principles of Human Reflexology.* London: Jarrolds Publishers.

Beck, A. T. (1967, 1978). *Depression.* Philadelphia: University of Pennsylvania Press.

Benedict, R. (1934, 1953). *Patterns of Culture.* New York: Mentor Books.

Bernstein, R. J. (1971). *Praxis & Action.* Philadelphia: University of Pennsylvania Press.

Berridge, K. C. and Grill, H. J. (1983). "Alternating ingestive and aversive consummatory responses suggest a two-dimensional analysis of palatability." *Behavioral Neuroscience,* 97: 563–573.

Bettelheim, B. (1980). *Surviving and Other Essays.* New York: Vintage Press.

Broca, P. (1861). "Remarks on the seat of the faculty of articulate language, followed by an observation of aphemia." In *Some Papers on the Cerebral Cortex*, Gerhardt Von Bonin (trans.). Springfield, IL: Charles C. Thomas (1960).

Brodal, A. (1981). *Neurological Anatomy*. New York: Oxford University Press.

Brush, A. D. and Halpern, B. P. (1971). "Centrifugal control of gustatory responses." *Physiology and Behavior*, 3: 713–718.

Buckley, P. (1986). *Essential Papers on Object Relations*. New York: New York University Press.

Burroughs, W. S. (1953, 1973). *Junky*. New York: Penguin Books.

C. Lasch. (1984). *The Minimal Self*. New York: Norton Press.

Cajal, S. R. (1911, 1960). "Anatomical and Physiological considerations about the brain." In Gerhardt Von Bonin, *Some Papers On The Cerebral Cortex*. Springfield, Illinois: Charles C. Thomas.

Camus, A. (1972). *The Plague*. New York: Vintage Press.

Carey, S. and Diamond, R. (1983). "From Piecemeal to configurational representation of faces." *Science*, 195: 312–314.

Carnap, R. (1928, 1969). *The Logical Structure of the World* (trans. by R. A. George). Berkeley and Los Angeles: University of California Press.

Cheng, K. (1986). "A purely geometric module in the rat's spatial representation." *Cognition*, 149–178.

Chomsky, N. (1965). *Aspects Of the Theory Of Syntax*. Cambridge: MIT Press

Chomsky, N. (1972). *Language and Mind*. New York: Harcourt Brace Jovanovich.

Churchland, P. M. (1979). *Scientific Realism and the Plasticity of Mind*. England: Cambridge University Press.

Churchland, P. S. (1986). *Neurophilosophy, Toward a Unified Science of the Mind-Brain*. Cambridge, Massachusetts: Bradford Book, MIT Press.

Coghill, G. E. (1929). *Anatomy and The Problem of Behavior*. Cambridge: Cambridge University Press.

Darwin, C. (1859, 1958). *The Origin of Species*. New York: Mentor Books.

Darwin, C. (1879, 1965). *The Expression of the Emotions in Man and Animals*. Chicago: University of Chicago.

Davidson, R. J. (1984). "Affect, cognition and hemispheric specialization." In *Emotions, Cognition and Behavior*. Edited by C. E. Izard, J. Kagan, and R. Zajonc. New York: Cambridge University Press.

Delza, S. (1961, 1985). *T'ai-Chi Ch'uan*. Albany: SUNY Press.

Dennett, D. C. (1969). *Content and Consciousness*. London: Routledge & Kegan Paul Ltd.

Dennett, D. C. (1978). *Brainstorms*. Cambridge: Bradford Books.

Dennett, D. C. (1984). "Cognitive Wheels: The Frame Problem of AI." In *Mind, Machines & Evolution*. Edited by C. Hooknay. Cambridge Univ. Press.

Dennett, D. C. (1985). *Elbow Room, The Varieties of Free Will Worth Wanting*. Cambridge: MIT Press.

Denton, D. A. (1982). *The Hunger for Salt*. New York: Springer-Verlag.

Dequincey, T. (1821, 1976). *Confessions of an English Opium Eater*. New York: Penguin Books.

DeRubeis, R. and Beck, A. T. (1988). "Cognitive Therapy." In *Handbook of Cognitive Behavior Therapy*. Edited by K. S. Dobson. New York: Guilford Press.

Des Pres, T. (1977). *The Survivor*. New York: Pocket Books.

Descartes, R. (1663, 1967). *Discourse on Method and Meditations*. (transl. by L. Lafleur). Indianapolis: Bobbs-Mettill Co.

Dewey, J. (1910). *How We Think*. New York: D.C. Heath & Company.

Dewey, J. (1910, 1965). *The Influence of Darwin on Philosophy*. Bloomington, Indiana: Indiana University Press.

Dewey, J. (1916). *Essays in Experimental Logic*. Chicago: Univ. of Chicago Press.

Dewey, J. (1916). *Democracy and Education*. Chicago: Univ. of Chicago Press.

Dewey, J. (1920, 1948). *Reconstruction in Philosophy*. Boston: Beacon Press.

Dewey, J. (1922, 1950). *Human Nature and Conduct*. New York: Modern Library, Random House.

Dewey, J. (1925, 1989). *Experience and Nature*. LaSalle Ill: Open Court.

Dewey, J. (1938). *Logic: The Theory of Inquiry*. New York: Holt Rinehart.

Dewey, J. (1929). *The Quest for Certainty*. New York: G. P. Putnam Sons.

Dewey, J. (1934, 1958). *Art as Experience*. New York: Capricorn Books.

Dewey, J. (1939). *Theory of Valuation*. Chicago: Univ. of Chicago Press.

Dewey, J. (1952). *Experience and Education*. New York: Collier Books.

Dickinson, A. (1980). *Contemporary Animal Learning Theory*. New York: Cambridge University Press.

Edelman, G. M. (1987). *Neural Darwinism*. New York: Basic Books.

Edwards, J. (1754, 1969). *Freedom of the Will*. Edited by A. S. Kaufman and W. K. Frankena. New York: The Bobbs-Merrill Co.

Ekman, P. (1972). "Universals and cultural differences in facial expressions of emotion." In *Nebraska Symposium on Motivations*. Edited by J. Cole, Vol. 19, pp. 207–283. Lincoln: University of Nebraska Press.

Eldredge, N. (1985). *Time Frames*. New York: Simon & Schuster.

Elster, J. (1979). *Ulysses and the Sirens*. Cambridge: Cambridge University Press.

Elster, J. (1983). *Sour Grapes*. Cambridge: Cambridge University Press.

Emerson, R. W. (1958). *A Modern Anthology*. New York: Dell Publishing.

Epstein, A. N. (1982). "Instinct and Motivation as explanations for complex behavior." In *The Physiological Mechanisms of Motivation* Edited by Pfaff, pp. 25–55. New York: Springer-Verlag.

Erikson, E. H. (1950, 1963). *Childhood and Society.* New York: W. W. Norton & Co.

Evarts, E. V. (1975). "Changing Concepts of the Central Control of Movement." *Canadian Journal of Physiology,* 53: 191–201.

Fairbairn, W. R. D. (1963). "Synopsis of an object-relations theory of personality." *International Journal of Psychoanalysis,* 44: 224–226.

Feigl, H. (1967). *The Mental and the Physical.* Minneapolis: University of Minnesota Press.

Ferrier, D. (1876). *The Functions of The Brain.* London: Smith, Elder, & Co.

Feuerbach, L. (1843, 1986). *Principles of the Philosophy of the Future.* (transl. by M. Fogel). Indianapolis: Hackett Publishing Company.

Fingarette, H. (1965). *The Self in Transformation.* New York: Harper Books.

Flechsig, P. E. (1905, 1960). "Brain physiology and theories of volition." In Gerhardt Von Bonin, *Some Papers On The Cerebral Cortex.* Springfield, Illinois: Charles C. Thomas.

Flourens, P. (1824, 1960). "Investigations of the properties and the functions of the various parts which compose the cerebral mass." In Gerhardt Von Bonin, *Some Papers On The Cerebral Cortex.* Springfield, Illinois: Charles C. Thomas.

Flower, E. & Murphy, M. G. (1977). *A History of Philosophy in America.* New York: Capricorn Books.

Flynn, J. P. (1972). "Patterning mechanisms, patterned reflexes, and attack behavior in cats." *Nebraska Symposium on Motivation,* 20: 125–153.

Fodor, J. A. (1979). *The Language of Thought.* Cambridge: Harvard University Press.

Fodor, J. A. (1981). "The Mind-Body Problem." *Scientific American,* 1: 124–133.

Fodor, J. A. (1983). *The Modularity of Mind.* Cambridge: MIT Press.

Frankfurt, H. G. (1988). *The Importance of What We Care About.* New York: Cambridge University Press.

Frankl, V. (1967). *Psychotherapy and Existentialism.* New York: Washington Square Press.

Franklin, B. (1987). *Essays, Articles, Bagatelles and Letters, Poor Richard's Almanac, Autobiography.* N.Y. Library of America.

Freud, S. (1924, 1960). *A General Introduction to Psychoanalysis.* (transl. by J. Riviere). New York: Washington Square Press (1960).

Freud, S. (1930, 1962). *Civilization and its Discontents* (transl. by J. Strachey). New York: W. W. Norton & Co.

Von-Frish, L. (1953). *The Dancing Bees.* New York: Harvest/HBJ.

Fromm, E. (1941). *Escape From Freedom.* New York: Holt, Rinehart and Company.

Fromm, E. (1947). *Man for Himself.* New York: Holt, Rinehart and Company.

Fromm E. (1956, 1974). *The art of loving.* New York: Harper and Row.

Fromm, E., Suzuki, D. T., and DeMartino, R. (1960). *Zen Buddhism and Psychoanalysis.* New York: Harper and Row.

Gadamer, H. G. (1960, 1985). *Truth and Method.* New York: Crossroad Publishing Company.

Gall, F. J. and Spurzheim, J. C. (1835). *On the functions of the brain and of each of its parts: with observations on the possibility of determining the instincts, propensities, and talents, or the moral and intellectual dispositions of men and animals, by the configuration of the brain and head* (transl. by W. Lewis, Jr). Boston: Marsh, Capen and Lyon.

Gallistel, C. R. (1980). *The Organization of Action: A New Synthesis.* Hillside, New Jersey: Lawrence Earlbaum Associates.

Gallistel, C. R. (1990). *The Organization of Learning.* Cambridge: MIT Press.

Gazzaniga, M. S. (1985). *The Social Brain.* New York: Basic Books.

Gelman, R. and Gallistel, C. R. (1978). *The Child's Concept of Number.* Cambridge: Harvard University Press.

Geschwind, N. (1980). "Neurological knowledge and complex behaviors." *Cognitive Science*, 4: 198–193.

Geschwind, N. and Levitzky, W. (1968). "Human brain: Left-right asymmetries in temporal speech region." *Science*, 161: 186–189.

Geschwind, N. (1964, 1974). "The development of the brain and the evolution of language." In *Selected Papers on Language and the Brain*. Boston: D. Reidel Publishing Co.

Geschwind, N. (1965, 1974). "Disconnection syndromes in animals and man." In *Selected Papers on Language and the Brain*. Boston: D. Reidel Publishing.

Gibson, J. J. (1966). *The Senses Considered as Perceptual Systems*. New York: Houghton-Mifflin.

Goffman, E. (1961). *Asylums*. New York: Anchor Books.

Goffman, E. (1971). *Relations in Public*. New York: Harper & Row.

Goldstein, K. (1939). *The Organism*. A Holistic Approach To Biology Derived From Pathological Data In Man. New York: American Book Co.

Goldstein, K. (1944). "The mental changes due to frontal lobe damage." *The Journal of Psychology*, 17: 187–208.

Goltz, F. (1888, 1978). "On the function of the hemispheres." In *The Cerebral Cortex*. Edited and transl. by G. Von Bonin. Springfield, ILL: Charles C. Thomas.

Goodman, N. (1955, 1973). *Fact, Fiction, and Forecast*. New York: Bobbs-Merrill Co.

Goy, R. W. and McEwen, B. S. (1980). *Sexual Differentiation of the Brain*. Cambridge: MIT Press.

Gray, J. C. (1967). *Warrior*. New York: Harper and Row.

Gregory, R. L. (1978). *Eye and Brain, The Psychology of Seeing*. New York: McGraw-Hill.

Grice, P. (1957). "Meaning." *Philosophical Review*.

Griffin, D. (1974). *Listening in the dark*. New York: Dover Publications.

Grill, H. J., Schulkin, J., and Flynn, F. W. (1986). "Sodium homeostasis in chronic decerebrate rats." *Behavioral Neuroscience*, 100(4): 536–543.

Guntrip, H. (1971). *Psychoanalytic Theory, Therapy, and the Self.* New York: Basic Books

Habermas, J. (1971). *Knowledge and Human Interests* (transl. by J. J. Shapiro). Boston: Beacon Press.

Habermas, J. (1973). *Theory and Practice* (transl. by J. Viertel). Boston: Beacon Press.

Habermas, J. (1975). *Legitimation Crisis* (transl. by T. McCarthy), Boston: Beacon Press.

Hacking, I. (1965). *Logic of Statistical Inference.* Cambridge: Cambridge University Press.

Hanson, N. R. (1958, 1972). *Patterns of Discovery.* Cambridge: Cambridge University Press.

Hartshorne, C. (1958). *Some biological principles applicable to song-behavior,* 70: 41–56. Wilson Bull.

Hebb, D. O. (1949). *The Organization of Behavior: A Neuropsychological Theory.* New York: John Wiley & Sons.

Hebb, D. O. (1959). "Intelligence, brain function and the theory of mind." *Brain*, 82: 260–275.

Heelan, P. A. (1983). *Space Perception and the Philosophy of Science.* Berkeley: Univ. of California Press.

Heidegger, M. (1972). *What is Called Thinking?* (transl. by F. D. Wieck and J. G. Gray). New York: Harper & Row.

Heidegger, M. (1973). *The End of Philosophy* (transl. by F. D. Wieck and J. G. Gray). New York: Harper & Row.

Hempel, C. B. (1965). *Aspects of Scientific Explanation.* New York: The Free Press.

Herrick, C. J. (1924, 1962). *Neurological Foundations of Animal Behavior.* New York: Hafner Publishers.

Herrick, C. J. (1926, 1967). *Brains of Rats And Men.* New York: Hafner Publishers.

Herrick, C. J. (1929). "Anatomical Patterns and Behavior Patterns." *Physiological Zoology*, 4: 439–448.

Hess, W. R. (1948, 1957). *The Functional Organization of The Diencephalon*. New York: Orange & Stratton, 1957.

Hobbes, I. (1651, 1958). *Leviathan*. New York: Bobbs-Merrill Co.

Hoffer, M. A. (1981). *The Roots of Human Behavior*. San Francisco: Freeman & Company.

Von Holst, E. (1969, 1973). *The Behavioral Physiology of Animals and Man*, Volume 1 (translated by R. Martin). Coral Gables, Florida: University of Miami Press, 1973.

Hubel, D. H. and Wiesel, T. H. (1972). "Laminar and columnar distribution of geniculocortical fibers in the macaque monkey." *Journal of Comparative Neurology*, 146: 421–450.

Husserl, E. (1929, 1973). *Cartesian Meditations, An Introduction to Phenomenology* (trans. by D. Cairns). Martinus Nijhoff, The Hague.

Izard, C. E. (1977). *Human Emotions*. New York: Plenum Press.

James, W. (1890, 1950). *The Principles of Psychology*, vol. 1 and 2. New York: Dover Publications.

James, W. (1899, 1958). *Talks to Teachers*. New York: Norton Press.

James, W. (1912, 1958). *Essays in Radical Empiricism*. New York: Longman, Green and Co.

James, W. (1907, 1959). *Pragmatism*. New York: Meridian Books.

James, W. (1896, 1956). *The Will to Believe Human Immortality and other Essays in Popular Philosophy*. New York: Dover Press.

James, W. (1902, 1974). *The Varieties of Religious Experience*. New York: Collier Macmillan Publishing Co.

James, W. (1910, 1970). *Pragmatism and other Essays*. New York: Washington Square Press.

Jefferson, T. (1939). *Thomas Jefferson on Democracy* (selected by S. K. Padover). New York: Mentor Books, D. Appleton-Century Col.

Jennings, H. J. (1905, 1962). *Behavior of The Lower Organisms*. Bloomington, Indiana: Indiana University Press.

Jerison, H. J. (1973). *Evolution of the Brain and Intelligence*. New York: Academic Press.

Kahneman, D. and Tversky, A. (1973). "On the Psychology of Prediction." *Psychological Review*. 80: 237–251.

Kandel, E. R. (1976). *Cellular Basis of Behavior*. San Francisco, California: W. H. Freeman & Co.

Kandel, E. R. & Schwartz, J. H. (1981). *Principles of Neural Science.* Holland, New York: Elsevier North.

Kant, I. (1787, 1965). *Critique of Pure Reason* (transl. by N. K. Smith). New York: St. Martin's Press.

Kant, I. (1788, 1956). *Critique of Practical Reason* (transl. by L. W. Beck). New York: Bobbs-Merrill Co.

Kant, I. (1790, 1951). *Critique of Judgement* (transl. by J. H. Barnard), New York: Hafner Press.

Kappers, C. U. A., Huber, G. C. and Crosby, E. C. (1967). *The Comparative Anatomy of the Nervous System of Vertebrates, Including Man,* volumes 1, 2, and 3. New York: Hafner Publishing Co.

Kegan, R. (1982). *The Evolving Self.* Cambridge: Harvard University Press.

Kelley, A. E., Domesick, V. B. & Nauta, W. J. H. (1982). "The amygdalostriatal projection in the rat—an anatomical study by anterograde and retrograde tracing methods." *Neuroscience,* 7: 615–630.

Kierkegaard, S. (1844, 1941). *Fear and Trembling and the Sickness Unto Death* (transl. by W. Lowrie). Princeton: Princeton University Press.

Kierkegaard, S. (1848, 1941). *Concluding Unscientific Postscript* (transl. by D. F. Swenson). Princeton: Princeton University Press.

Kirk, G. S. and Raven, J. E. (1957). *The Presocratic Philosophers.* Cambridge: Cambridge University Press.

Klein, M. (1932, 1975). *Psychoanalysis of Children* (transl. by Streicke). New York: Delta Publishers.

Kluver, Heinrich, and Bucy, P. C. (1939). "Preliminary analysis of functions of the temporal lobes in monkeys." *Archives of Neurology and Psychology,* 42: 979–1000.

Kohler, W. (1925). *The Mentality of Apes.* London: Routledge & Kegan Paul.

Kohut, H. (1985). *Self Psychology and the Humanities.* New York: W.W. Norton & Company.

Konorski, J. (1967). *Integrative Activity of the Brain, An Interdisciplinary Approach.* Chicago: University of Chicago Press.

Korczak, J. C. (1978). *Ghetto Diary.* New York: Holocaust Library.

Krieckhaus, E. E. and Ekikson, C. W. (1960). "A study of awareness and its effect on learning and generalization." *Journal of Personality,* 28: 503–517.

Kripke, S. A. (1982). *Wittgenstein, on Rules and Private Language.* Cambridge: Harvard University Press.

Kuhn, T. S. (1962). *The Structure of Scientific Revolutions.* Chicago: University of Chicago Press.

Lamark, J. B. (1809, 1984). *Zoological Philosophy* (transl. by H. Elliot). Chicago: University of Chicago Press.

Langer, K. (1957). *Problems of Art.* New York: Charles Scribner's Sons.

Laqueur, W. (1982). *The Terrible Secret.* New York: Penquin Press.

Lasch, C. (1984). *The Minimal Self.* New York: Norton Press.

Lashley, K. S. (1929). *Brain Mechanisms and Intelligence.* Chicago: University of Chicago Press.

Lashley, K. S. (1950, 1960). "In search of the engram." *The Neuropsychology of Lashley: Selected Papers of K. S. Lashley.* Edited by F. A. Beach, D. O. Hebb, C. T. Morgan & H. A. Nissen. New York: McGraw-Hill.

Lashley, K. S. (1958, 1960). "Cerebral organization of behavior." *The Neuropsychology of Lashley: Selected Papers of K. S. Lashley.* Edited by F. A. Beach, D. O. Hebb, C. T. Morgan and H. A. Nissen. New York: McGraw-Hill.

Lenneberg, E. H. (1967). *Biological Foundations of Language.* New York: Wiley.

Levi-Strauss. (1985). *The View From Afar.* New York: Basic Books.

Lewis, C. I. (1929, 1956). *Mind and the World Order.* New York: Dover Publications.

Lewis, C. I. (1946). *An Analysis of Knowledge and Valuation.* LaSalle: Open Court.

Lieberman, P. (1984). *The Biology and Evolution of Language.* Cambridge, Mass.: Harvard University Press.

Locke, J. (1690, 1959). *An Essay Concerning Human Understanding*, vol. One and Two. Collated and annotated by A. C. Fraser. New York: Dover Press.

Loeb, J. (1900, 1973). *Comparative Physiology of The Brain*. New York: Arno Press.

Loeb, J. (1918, 1973). *Forced Movements, Tropisms, and Animal Conduct*. New York: Dover Publications.

Lorente de No. R. (1938). "Cerebral cortex: Architecture, intracortical connections, motor projections." In *Physiology of the Nervous System*. Edited by J. F. Fulton. New York: Oxford University Press.

Luria, A. R. (1973). *The Working Brain, An Introduction to Neuropsychology* (transl. by B. Haigh). New York: Basic Books.

McCelland, J. L. & Rumelhart, D. E. (1986). *Parallel Distributed Processing*. Boston: Bradford MIT Press.

Machiavelli, N. (1952). *The Prince* (transl. by L. Ricci, revised by E. R. P. Vincent). New York: Mentor Book from New American Library.

McFarland, D. J. (1977). "Decision making in animals." *Nature*, 269: 15–20.

Mackintosh, N. J. (1975). "A theory of attention: Variations of associability of stimuli with reinforcers." *Psychological Review*, 82: 276–298.

MacLean, P. D. (1949). "Psychosomatic disease and the 'visceral brain.'" *Psychosomatic Medicine*, 11: 338–353.

Macphail, E. M. (1982). *Brain and Intelligence in Vertebrates*. Oxford: Clarendon Press.

Mahler, M. S., Pine, F., and Bergman, A. (1975). *The Psychological Birth of the Human Infant*. New York: Basic Books.

Maimonides, M. (1975). *Ethical Writings of Maimonides*. Edited by L. Weiss with C. Butterworth. New York: Dover Press.

Marler, R. and Hamilton, W. J. III. (1966). *Mechanisms of Animal Behavior*. New York: John Wiley and Sons, Inc.

Marr, D. (1981). "Artificial intelligence." In *Mind Design*. Edited by J. Haugeland. Boston: Bradford MIT Press.

Marr, D. (1982). *Vision.* San Francisco: W. H. Freeman & Co.

Mason, K. (1974). *Dance Therapy.* American Association for Health, Physical Education and Recreation. 1201 Sixteenth St., Washington, D.C.

Maugham, W. S. (1915). *Of Human Bondage.* New York: Doubleday.

Mead, G. H. (1934). *Mind, Self and Society.* Chicago: Univ. of Chicago Press.

Mead, G. H. (1938, 1972). *The Philosophy of the Act.* Chicago: Univ. of Chicago Press.

Mead, M. (1928). *Coming of Age in Samoa.* New York: William Morrow and Co.

Merleau-Ponty, M. (1964). *The Primacy of Perception* (transl. by J. M. Edie). Edited by J. M. Edie. Evanston: Northwestern University Press.

Meyer, L. (1956). *Emotion and Meaning in Music.* Chicago: University of Press.

Milgram, S. (1975). *Obedience to Authority.* New York: Harper Press.

Mill, J. (1843, 1873). *A system of logic.* London: Longsmans, Green, Rader and Dyer.

Miller, A. (1981). *The Drama of the Gifted Child* (transl. by R. Ward). New York: Basic Books.

Miller, F. R. and Sherrington, C. S. (1916). "Some observations on the bucco-pharyngeal stage of reflex deglutition in the cat." *Quarterly Journal of Experimental Physiology,* 9: 147–186.

Milner, B. (1972). "Disorders of learning and memory after temporal-lobe lesions in man." *Clinical Neurosurgery,* 19: 421–446.

Mishkin M. (1982). "A memory system in the monkey." *Philosophical Transactions of the Royal Society of London,* 298: 85–95.

Mishkin, M., Malamut, B. and Bahevalier, J. (1984). "Memories and habits." In *Neurobiology of Learning and Memory.* Edited by G. Lynch, J. McGaugh and N. Weinberger. New York: Guilford Press.

Morris, C. (1938). *Foundations of the Theory of Signs.* Chicago: Univ. of Chicago Press.

Mountcastle, V. B. (1964). "The neural replication of sensory events in the somatic afferent system." *Brain and Conscious Experience.* Edited by J. C. Eccles. New York: Springer-Verlag.

Mountcastle, V. B. (1978). "An organizing principle for cerebral function: The unit module and the distributed system." In Edelman, G. M. & Mountcastle, V. B., *The Mindful Brain.* Cambridge: MIT Press.

Mountcastle, V. B. (1978). "Some neural mechanisms for directed attention." *Inserm symposium No. 6,* Buser and Rougeul Buser, Elsevier/North Holland Biomedical Press.

Munk, Hermann. (1881, 1960). "On the functions of the cortex." In Gerhardt Von Bonin, *Some Papers on the Cerebral Cortex.* Springfield, Illinois: Charles C. Thomas, 1960.

Nagel, T. (1979). *Mortal questions.* New York: Cambridge University Press.

Nagel, T. (1986). *The View from Nowhere.* Oxford: Oxford University Press.

Nauta, W. J. H. & Karten, H. J. (1970). "A general profile of the vertebrate brain, with sidelights on the ancestry of cerebral cortex." In *The Neurosciences.* (F. O. Schmitt, editor-in-chief). New York: Rockefeller University Press.

Neville, R. C. (1974). *The Cosmology of Freedom.* New Haven: Yale University Press.

Neville, R.C. (1978). *Soldier, Sage, Saint.* New York: Fordham University Press.

Neville, R. C. (1981). *Reconstruction of Thinking.* Albany: SUNY Press.

Neville, R. C. (1983). *Axiology of Thinking.* Albany: SUNY Press.

Neville, R. C. (1987). *The Puritan Smile.* Albany: SUNY Press.

Neville, R. C. (1989). *Recovery of the Measure.* Albany: SUNY Press.

Nietzsche, F. (1882, 1960). *Joyful Wisdom.* New York: Frederick Ungar Publishing Co.

Nietzsche, F. (1886, 1966). *Beyond good and evil* (transl. by W. Kaufman). New York: Vantage Books.

Norgren, R. and Grill, H. J. (1982). "Brainstem control of ingestive behavior. In *The Physiology of Motivation*, edited by D. Pfaff, pp. 99–131. New York: Springer-Verlag.

Nottebohm, F. (1980). "Brain pathways for vocal learning in birds." *Progress in Psychobiology and Physiological Psychology*, edited by A. Epstein & J. Sprague. New York: Academic Press.

Nowlis, G. H. (1977). "From reflex to representation: taste-elicited tongue movements in the human newborn." *Taste and Development*. Edited by J. M. Weiffenbach. Bethesda, Maryland: U.S. Department of Health, Education, and Welfare.

Oakley, D. A. (1979). "Learning with food reward and shock avoidance in neodecorticate rats." *Experimental Neurology*, 63: 627–642.

Olton, D. (1982). "Spatially organized behaviors of animals: Behavioral and neurological studies." In *Spatial Abilitites: Development and Physiological Foundations*. Edited by M. Potegal. New York: Academic Press

Papez, J. (1937). "A proposed mechanism of emotion." *Archives of Neurology And Psychiatry*, 38: 725–743.

Parrott, G. A. and Schulkin, J. (1992). "Neuropsychology and the Cognitive Nature of the Emotions." *Cognition and Emotion*, in press.

Pavlov, I. P. (1927). *Conditioned Reflexes* (transl. by G. V. Anrep). New York: Dover Publications.

Peirce, C. S. (1877). "The fixation of belief." *Popular Science Monthly*, 12: 1–15.

Peirce, C. S. (1887). "Logical Machines." *Am. Journal of Psychology*, 1: 165–170.

Peirce, C. S. (1878). "How to make our ideas clear." *Popular Science Monthly*, 12: 287–302.

Peirce, C. S. (1931, 1934). Collected Papers of Charles Sanders Peirce. C. Hartshorne and P. Weiss (Eds.). Cambridge, Massachusetts: Belknap Press Book, Harvard University Press.

Penfield, W. (1959). "The interpretive cortex." *Science*, 129: 1719–1725.

Pfaff, D. W. (1980). *Estrogens and Brain Function: Neural Analysis of a Hormone-Controlled Mammalian Reproductive Behavior.* New York: Springer-Verlag.

Piaget, J. (1972). *The Child and Reality* (transl. by A. Rosin). New York: Penguin Books.

Plato (1956). *Great Dialogues of Plato* (trans. by W. H. D. Rouse). Edited by E. H. Warmington and P. G. Rouse. New York: Mentor Book from New American Library.

Premack, D. (1976). *Intelligence in Ape and Man.* Hillsdale, New Jersey: Lawrence Erlbaum Associates.

Premack, D. and Premack, A. J. (1983). *The Mind of an Ape.* New York: Norton Press.

Quine, W. V. O. (1960). *Word and Object.* Cambridge: MIT Press.

Quine, W. V. O. (1969). *Ontological Relativity & Other Essays.* New York: Columbia University Press.

Quine, W. V. O. (1976). *The Ways of Paradox and Other Essays.* Cambridge: Harvard University Press.

Rawls, J. (1971). *A Theory of Justice.* Cambridge, Mass.: Belknap Press of Harvard University Press.

Rescorla, R. A. (1972). "Informational Variables in Pavlovian Conditioning." In *Psychology of Learning and Motivation*, Vol. 6. Edited by G. Bower. New York: Academic Press.

Rescorla, R. A. (1978). "Some implications of a cognitive perspective on Pavlovian conditioning." In *Cognitive Aspects of Animal Behavior*, edited by H. Fowler, W. K. Honig, and S. Hulse. Hillsdale, New Jersey: Erlbaum Publishers.

Rey, G. (1980). "Functionalism and the emotions." E. O. Rorty (Ed.). *Explaining the Emotions.* Berkeley California: University of California Press.

Ribbot, T. (1882). *Diseases of Memory.* New York: Appleton Century Crofts.

Ricardo, J. A. & Koh, E. T. (1978). "Anatomical evidence of direct projections from the nucleus of the solitary tract to the hypothalamus, amygdala, and other forebrain structures in the rat." *Brain Research*, 153: 1–26.

Richter, C. P. (1965, 1979). *Biological Clocks in Medicine and Psychiatry*. Springfield, Illinois: Charles C. Thomas.

Ricketts, T. G. (1982). "Rationality, Translation and Epistemology Naturalized." *Journal of Philosophy* 3: 117–130.

Ricketts, T. G. (1985). "The Tractatus, and the Logocentric Predicament." *Nous*, 19: 1–16.

Rieff, P. (1966). *The Triumph of the Therapeutic*. New York: Harper & Row.

Rogers, C. R. (1961). *On Becoming a Person*. Boston: Houghton Mifflin Co.

Romer, A. S. (1970). *The Vertebrate Body*. Philadelphia: W. B. Saunders.

Rorty, R. (1979). *Philosophy and the Mirror of Nature*. Princeton, New Jersey: Princeton University Press.

Rorty, R. (1982). *Consequence of Pragmatism*. Minneapolis: Univ. of Minnesota Press.

Rorty, R. (1989). *Contingency, Irony and Solidarity*. Cambridge: Cambridge, Press.

Rorty, R. (1991). *Philosophical Papers*, Vol. 1 & 2. Cambridge: Cambridge University Press.

Rosenwasser, A. M. and Adler, N. T. (1986). "Structure and function in circadian timing systems: Evidence for multiple coupled circadian oscillators." *Neuroscience & Biobehavioral Reviews*, 10: 431–448.

Rousseau, J. J. (1755, 1984). *A Discourse on Inequality* (transl. by M. Cranston). New York: Penguin Press.

Rozin, P. (1976). "The evolution of intelligence and access to the cognitive unconscious." In J. M. Sprague & A. N. Einstein (Eds.), *Progress In Physiological Psychology*, Vol 6. New York: Academic Press.

Rozin, P. (1976). "The psychobiological approach to human memory." In *Neural Mechanisms of Learning and Memory*. Edited by M. R. Rosenzweig and E. L. Bennett. Cambridge, MA: MIT Press.

Rozin, P. and Schulkin, J. (1990). "Food selection." *Handbook of Food and Fluid Intake*. Edited by E. M. Stricker. New York: Plenum Press.

Ryle, G. (1959). *The Concept of Mind*. New York: Harper and Row.

Sabini, J. and Schulkin, J. (1990). "Some Mind-Body issues in contemporary psychology." Unpublished manuscript.

Sabini, J. and Silver, M. (1982). *Moralities of Everyday Life*. New York: Oxford University Press.

Sabini, J. and Silver, M. (1985). "On the captivity of the will: Sympathy, caring, and a moral sense of the human." *Journal for the Theory of Social Behavior*, 15: 23–36.

Sachs, C. (1937). *World History of Dance*. p. 139. New York: W. W. Norton Press.

Sartre, J. P. (1943, 1956). *Being and Nothingness* (transl. by H. E. Barnes). New York: Washington Square Press.

Sartre, J. P. (1948). *The Emotions: Outline of Theory* (transl. by H. E. Barnes). New York: Philosophical Library.

Satinoff, F. (1978). "Neural organization and evolution of thermal regulation in mammals." *Science*, 201: 16–27.

Schaffer, C. E. & Blatt, S. J. (1990). "Interpersonal relationships and the experience of perceived efficacy." In *Perceptions of Competence and Incompetence Across the Lifespan*, edited by J. Kolligian, Jr. and R. J. Sternberg.

Schaller, G. (1964). *The Year of the Gorilla*. Chicago: University of Chicago Press.

Schelling, F. W. J. (1809, 1936). *Philosophical Inquiries into the Nature of Human Freedom* (transl. by J. Gutmann). Illinois: Open Court.

Schiller, F. (1795, 1980). *On The Aesthetic Education of Man* (transl. by R. Snell). New York: Frederick Ungar Publishers.

Schneirla, T. C. (1959). "An evolutionary and developmental theory of biphasic process underlying approach and withdrawal." In L. R. Aronson, E. Tobach, J. S. Tobach, J. S. Rosenblatt, & D. S. Lehram (eds.), *Selected Writings Of T.C. Schneirla*. San Francisco, California: Freeman & Co.

Schopenhauer, A. (1839, 1985). *On the Freedom of the Will* (trans. by K. Kolenda). Oxford: Basil Blackwell.

Schulkin, J. (1989). *Preoperative Events: Their Effects on Behavior Following Brain Damage*. New Jershey: Erlbaum Press.

Schulkin, J. (1991). *Sodium Hunger: The Search for a Salty Taste.* Cambridge: Cambridge University Press.

Schulkin, J. and Neville, R. C. (1983). "Responsibility, Rehabilitation, and Drugs: Health care dilemmas." In *Ethical Problems in the Nurse-Patient Relationship.* Edited by C. P. Murphy and H. Hunter. Massachusetts: Allyn and Bacon.

Schwaber, J., Kapp, B. S., Higgens, G. A. and Rapp, P. R. (1982). "Amygdaloid and basal forebrain direct connections with the nucleus of the solitary tract and the dorsal motor nucleus." *Journal of Neuroscience,* 10: 1424–1438.

Searle, J. (1986). *Minds, Brains and Science.* Cambridge, Mass.: Harvard University Press.

Sellars, W. (1962). *Science, Perception and Reality.* London: Routledge and Kegan.

Sellars, W. (1968). *Science and Metaphysics.* New York: Humanities Press.

Sereny, G. (1983). *Into that Darkness: An Examination of Conscious.* New York: Vantage Books.

Schneider, H. W. (1946, 1967). *A History of American Philosophy.* New York: Columbia Univ. Press.

Setschenow, J. (1863). *Physiologische studien uber den hemmungmechanismus fur die reflexthatigkeit des ruckenmarkes und gehirnes der froschen.* Berlin, Hirschwald.

Sherington, C. (1906). *The Integrative Action of the Nervous System.* New Haven, Conn.: Yale University Press, 1961.

Shipley, M. T. and Sanders, M. S. (1982). "Special senses are really special: Evidence for a reciprocal, bilateral pathway between insular cortex and nucleus parabrachialis." *Brain Research Bulletin,* 8: 493–501.

Siegel, S. (1987). "Alcohol and opiate dependence: re-evaluation of the Victorian perspective." In *Research Advances in Alcohol and Drug Problems,* Vol. 9. Edited by H. Cappell, Y. Israel, H. Kalant, W. Schmidt, E. M. Sellers, & R. G. Smart. New York: Plenum Press.

Simon, H. (1969). *The Science of the Artificial.* Cambridge: MIT Press.

Smith, J. E. (1963). *The Spirit of American Philosophy*. Oxford: Oxford Univ. Press.

Smith, J. E. (1970). *Themes in American Philosophy*. New York: Harper & Row.

Smith, J. E. (1978). *Purpose and Thought*. New Haven: Yale Univ. Press.

Smith, J. E. (1987). "Being and willing: the foundation of ethics." *Journal of Speculative Philosophy*, 1: 24–37.

Smith, W. J. (1977). *The Behavior of Communicating*. Cambridge: Harvard University Press.

Solomon, R. C. (1988). *A History of Western Philosophy: Continental Philosophy Since 1750: The Rise and Fall of Self*. New York: Oxford University Press.

Spencer, H. (1880, 1901). *The Principles of Psychology*. New York: D. Appleton & Co.

Sperry, R. W. (1945). "The problem of central nervous reorganization after nerve regeneration and muscle transposition: A critical review." *Quarterly Review of Biology*, 20: 311–369.

Sperry, R. W. (1961). "Cerebral organization and behavior." *Science*, 133: 1749–1757.

Spinoza, B. (1668, 1955). *On the Improvement of the Understanding, The Ethics, Correspondence* (transl. by R. H. M. Elwes). New York: Dover Press.

Squire, L. R. (1987). *Memory and Brain*. New York: Oxford University Press.

Steiner, J. E. (1973). "The gusto-facial response: Observation on normal and anencephalic newborn infants." In *4th symposium on oral sensations and perception*. Edited by J. F. Bosmas. Washington, D.C.: U.S. Government Printing Office.

Stellar, E. (1954). "The Physiology of Motivation." *Psychological Review*, 61: 5–22.

Stellar, E. (1985). *Scientists and Human Rights in Chile*. National Academy of Sciences, Washington, D.C.

Stellar, J. R, and Stellar, E. (1985). *The Neurobiology of Motivation and Reward*. New York: Springer-Verlag.

Stelzner, D. J. (1986). "Ontogeny of the encephalization process." In *Developmental Neuropsychobiology.* Edited by W. T. Greenough & J. M. Juraska, pp. 241–270. New York: Academic Press.

Teitelbaum, P. (1967). *Physiological Psychology.* Englewood Cliffs, N.J.: Prentice-Hall.

Teitelbaum, P. (1971). "The encephalization of hunger." In *Progress in Physiological Psychology.* Edited by E. Stellar & J. Sprague, 4: 319–350.

Terreberry, R. R. & Neafsey, E. J. (1983). "Rat medial frontal cortex: a visceral motor region with a direct projection to the solitary nucleus." *Brain Research*, 278: 245–249.

Thompson, R. (1986). "The neurobiology of learning and memory." *Science*, 233:(4767): 941–947.

Thoreau, H. D. (1971). *Great Short Works.* New York: Harper & Row.

Tillich, P. (1952, 1974). *The Courage To Be.* New Haven: Yale University Press.

Tocqueville, A. (1848, 1945). *Democracy In America* (transl. by P. Bradley). New York: Vintage Books.

Towe, A. L. (1975). "Notes on the hypothesis of columnar organization in somatosensory cerebral cortex." *Brain, Behavior and Evolution*, 11: 16–47.

Turnball, C. (1981). "East African Safari." *Natural History*, Vol. 90, No. 5.

Vaillant, G. E. (1983). *The Natural History of Alcoholism.* Cambridge: Harvard University Press (1983).

Vico, G. (1710, 1988). *On the Most Ancient Wisdom of the Italians* (transl. by L. M. Palmer). Ithaca: Cornell University Press.

Vygotsky, L. S. (1936, 1979). *Thought and Language.* Cambridge: MIT Press.

Weber, M. (1947). *Social and Economic Organization.* Oxford: Oxford University Press.

Weisel, E. (1982). *Night.* New York: Bartram Books.

Weiss, P. (1958). *Modes of Being.* Evanston, Illinois: Southern Illinois University Press.

Weiss, P. A. (1939). *Principles of Development*. New York: Henry Holt.

Weissman, D. (1987). *Intuition and Ideality*. Albany: SUNY Press.

Wernicke, C. (1874). *Der Aphasische Symptomenkomplex*. Breslau: Cohn and Weigart.

Wheelis, A. (1973). *How People Change*. New York: Harper & Row

White, R. W. (1959). "Motivation reconsidered: The concept of competence." *Psychological Review*, 66(5): 297–333.

White, M. (1956). *Positivism and Pragmatism: Toward Reunion in Philosophy*. Cambridge: Harvard Univ. Press.

Whitehead, A. N. (1927, 1953). *Symbolism*. New York: Macmillan Company.

Whitehead, A. N. (1927, 1978). *Process and Reality*, Corrected Edition. Edited by D. R. Griffin and D. W. Sherburne. New York: Free Press, Macmillan Publishing Co.

Whitehead, A. N. (1929). *The Function of Reason*. New Jersey: Princeton University Press.

Whitehead, A. N. (1933, 1967). *Adventures of Ideas*. New York: Free Press.

Wiener, P. (1949). *Evolution and the Founders of Pragmatism*. Cambridge: Harvard Univ. Press.

Wiersma, C. A. G. (1967). *Invertebrate Nervous Systems*. Chicago: University of Chicago Press.

Wilson, E. O. (1975). *Sociobiology*. Cambridge: Harvard Univ. Press.

Winnicott, D. W. (1957, 1987). *The Child, the Family, and the Outside World*. Massachusetts: Addison-Wesley Publishing Co.

Wittgenstein, L. (1922, 1961). *Tractatus Logico-Philosophicus* (trans. D. F. Pears & B. F. McGuinness). London: Routledge & Kegan Paul.

Wittgenstein, L. (1953, 1968). *Philosophical Investigations* (transl. by G. E. M. Anscombe). New York: Macmillan Publishing Co.

Wolf, G. (1984). "The Place of the Brain in an Ocean of Feelings." In *Existence and Actuality: Conversations with Charles Hartshorne*. Edited by J. B. Cobb, Jr. and F. I. Gamwell. Chicago: University of Chicago Press.

Woodruff, G. and Premack, D. (1979). "Intentional Communication in the Chimpanzee: The Development of Deception." *Cognition*, 7: 333–362.

Wright, C. (1958). *Philosophical Writings*. New York: Liberal Arts Press.

Young, R. M. (1970). *Mind, Brain & Adaptation*. Oxford: Oxford University Press.

Index

193